DATE DUE

RIVERSIDE CITY COLLEGE
LIBRARY
Riverside, California

AG   '84

DEMCO

Opera
Guide

14

La
Bohème

Puccini

David Rendall as Rodolfo and Valerie Masterson as Mimì in the First Act of Jean-Claude Auvray's 1977 production for ENO (photo: Andrew March)

Preface

This series, published under the auspices of English National Opera and The Royal Opera, aims to prepare audiences to enjoy and evaluate opera performances. Each book contains the complete text, set out in the original language together with a current performing translation. The accompanying essays have been commissioned as general introductions to aspects of interest in each work. As many illustrations and musical examples as possible have been included because the sound and spectacle of opera are clearly central to any sympathetic appreciation of it. We hope that, as companions to the opera should be, they are well-informed, witty and attractive.

Nicholas John
Series Editor

14

La Bohème

Giacomo Puccini

Opera Guide Series Editor: Nicholas John

Published in association with English National Opera and The Royal Opera

John Calder · London
Riverrun Press · New York

Riverrun Press Inc.,
175 Fifth Avenue
New York, NY 10010

Copyright © English National Opera and The Royal Opera, 1982

Some Aspects of *La Bohème*
© William Ashbrook, 1982

Romance and Irony: A commentary on 'La Bohème'
© Nicholas John, 1982

Henry Murger and *La vie de Bohème*
©Joanna Richardson, 1982

The Music of 'La Bohème'
© Edward Greenfield, 1982

La Bohème: English version
© G. Ricordi & Co.

BRITISH LIBRARY CATALOGUING IN PUBLICATION DATA

Puccini, Giacomo
    La Bohème. — (Opera Guide; 14)
    1. Puccini, Giacomo.   La Bohème
    2. Operas — Librettos
    I. Title   II. John, Nicholas   III. Giacosa, Giuseppe   IV. Illica, Luigi   V. Series
    782.1′092′4   ML410.P89

ISBN 0 7145 3938 4

SUBSIDISED BY THE
Arts Council
OF GREAT BRITAIN

John Calder (Publishers) Ltd, English National Opera and
The Royal Opera House, Covent Garden Ltd receive financial
assistance from the Arts Council of Great Britain. English
National Opera also receives financial assistance from the
Greater London Council.

Typeset in Plantin by Margaret Spooner Typesetting, Dorchester, Dorset.

Printed and bound in Great Britain by Whitstable Litho Ltd., Whitstable, Kent.

Contents

List of Illustrations

Some Aspects of 'La Bohème'

William Ashbrook

When *La Bohème* was first introduced at New York's Metropolitan Opera House in December 1900 Henry Krehbiel started off his review of that event in these terms: '*La Bohème* is foul in subject, and fulminant but futile in its music'. Today when the esteem and affection with which *Bohème* is regarded are if anything firmer than ever, Krehbiel's alliterative dismissal seems ludicrously stuffy and wide of its mark. Yet among critics of that time Krehbiel's peevishness reflected a not uncommon attitude. In October 1897 when the Carl Rosa Company gave the opera its London première at Covent Garden, one reviewer dismissed the score as 'not stimulating enough to be heard often'. Even its first Italian audiences shared this resistance to what seems today to be the opera's inescapable appeal. This once widespread attitude provides a convenient way to approach *La Bohème* afresh, as a work very much of its period, symptomatic of its time.

The critics and general public attending the première of *La Bohème* at Turin's Teatro Regio on February 1, 1896, found themselves rather lost, not quite knowing how to relate to this novelty. One reason for this sense of disorientation lies in the context created by the operas that preceded it on the Regio's bill. That season had opened on December 22, 1895 with the Italian première of *Götterdämmerung*, conducted by Toscanini, and it would be repeated twenty times during the next months; interlarded in this run of *Götterdämmerung* were five performances of Verdi's *Falstaff*, opening on December 28; Verdi's final opera was not yet three years old, but this was its second 'edition' at Turin. Both *Götterdämmerung* and *Falstaff* were works that put the Turin public on its mettle because of their relative difficulty and novelty; the setting and action of both works were alien to the everyday world of proto-industrial Turin. Imagine the jolt, then, of *La Bohème* with its tenement studio and dowdy urban ambience after such fare, and consider too that as a comi-tragedy it presented an unfamiliar mixture of genres. Pucccini's combination of humorous and tragic elements must have puzzled an Italian public familiar with the old *semiseria* convention, which inserted *buffo* characters into serious plots that ended happily and which traditionally kept the comic and serious characters distinct. *La Bohème* involved a shrinking of the aesthetic distance from something as remote as the primeval banks of the Rhine to a smaller scale world populated by characters one might encounter on the streets of any large city, and it is precisely the adjustment of emotional perspective demanded by Puccini's opera that caused its first audiences to feel they had lost their bearings. But the initial coolness of the reception seems to have worn off quickly since some of the twenty-three performances that season were probably added to meet public demand.

The sense of immediacy or of universality produced by the drama of *La Bohème*, did not then fit handily into anyone's preconceptions of what operas were supposed to be about. Although its action was nominally set in the Paris of Louis-Philippe, it seemed closer in time and place because the poorer sections of large cities and the behaviour of artists and their girls are not redolent of any particular period. To think for a moment of the different effect produced by *La Bohème* in comparison to that by the Louis-Quinze flavour of

Evan Gorga, the first Rodolfo in Turin, 1896

Ines Maria Ferraris, the Musetta in the performance given at La Scala in 1925 to honour Puccini's memory.

Manon Lescaut (its immediate predecessor in Puccini's output) is to grasp the point. In 1896 audiences were unaccustomed to encountering in the operahouse something close to the world of the streets outside. Nor should the immediacy of *La Bohème* be confused with the naturalistic effusiveness of works like *Cavalleria* (1890) and *Pagliacci* (1892), for they involve crimes of passion carried out in a comparatively primitive setting. Undeniably there are elements in *La Bohème* conditioned by the *verismo* vogue – Mimi's pathetic catalogue of personal effects in her 'Farewell' is a case in point – but they have been adapted unobtrusively into a framework that seems almost sophisticated when set against that employed by Mascagni and Leoncavallo. Certainly *Pagliacci* also mixes comic and tragic ingredients in its plot, but there the stylized artificiality of the *commedia dell'arte* performed by Canio's troupe supplies a needed change of pace to the intensities of the main action, while the humour of *La Bohème* involves the 'gay yet terrible' lives of the characters themselves – to quote a tag from Murger prefixed to Puccini's score.

Tradition has it that the seal of unqualified acceptance was set upon Puccini's opera when it was introduced to Palermo in April 1896, after the composer had made a number of slight but crucial adjustments to his score. Though the opera soon made its way, its early performers were called upon to find a tone and a mode of acting unlike anything demanded by their previous stage experience. Further, *La Bohème* called out to a segment of the urban public beyond the restricted circle that customarily patronized the opera house, for people could indentify with Rodolfo, Mimi and Marcello, and their desire for warmth, love and high spirits, more closely than with an Ernani or an Azucena. And this new public was no more used to encountering its counterparts upon the lyric stage than were subscribers of long-standing. Nearly twenty years after the première of *La Bohème* Ildebrando Pizzetti would lambaste Puccini's art as 'bourgeois', and however sincere this rival

8

composer's rancour at the gravitational pull exerted upon the repertory by works like *La Bohème*, he put his finger directly upon its most novel aspect. The mid–1890s were a time of real social unrest in the industrial cities of Northern Italy like Turin, where the Labour movement held some of its first work stoppages in Italy during those years, and to some extent *Bohème*, with its more democratic appeal, its (admittedly romanticized) depiction of poverty ('*Ah, la miseria!*'), was a sign of these changing times.

Bohemianism, as described in the opera's sources, Henri Murger's prose sketches and his later dramatization of them (in collaboration with Théodore Barrière), was a subject that exerted a personal attraction upon Puccini. As a student at the Milan Conservatory graduating in 1883, Puccini had first-hand knowledge of both the gaiety and grimness of *la vie de Bohème*. It is largely a waste of time, however, to dig for exact parallels of the plot of *La Bohème* in Puccini's own experience, since his co-librettists, Giuseppe Giacosa and Luigi Illica, demonstrably based their text upon an amalgam of characters and episodes in their sources; more fruitful would be a brief glance at Bohemianism as a phenomenon of Northern Italian life. It did not really take root in Milan until the 1860s, delayed because the *Risorgimento* and subsequent Unification had demanded a different style of demeanour, but once these patriotic questions were settled and the old fervours had become tinged with some disillusion, there arose a group of writers, painters and composers in Milan who called themselves the *Scapigliatura* (the Disorderly Ones). As a movement it was relatively short-lived: their *pronunciamenti* about new directions for art received a humiliating setback with the initial fiasco of Boito's *Mefistofele* in 1868, since Boito had for a time been in the forefront of the *Scapigliati*. But if the accomplishments of that group seem wayward and shallow in retrospect, the influence exerted by the movement upon the youth of that time and later was more lasting, and it gave an air of modishness to what might otherwise have seemed mere exuberance. To one who, like

Maria Zamboni as Mimì (Teatro alla Scala)

Aureliano Pertile as Rodolfo, a role he sang at La Scala and Covent Garden in the late 1920s (Teatro alla Scala)

9

An early production of Act Two in Berlin featuring Florence Easton as Musetta and Frieda Hempel as Mimi. (Raymond Mander and Joe Mitchenson Theatre Collection)

Puccini, had immersed himself in this influence, Murger's vignettes had the force of prototypes.

The writing of the libretto of *La Bohème* was entrusted by Giulio Ricordi, with Puccini's acquiescence, to Giacosa and Illica. Ricordi had brought them together as a team to put the final touches and adjustments on the troublesome libretto of *Manon Lescaut*, adjusting a work that had seen a number of people (Leoncavallo, Mario Praga, Domenico Oliva, and both Puccini and Ricordi) turn their hands to it. Giuseppe Giacosa (1847–1906) had up to this time been primarily a dramatist and poet; while Luigi Illica (1857–1919) was primarily a librettist, writing among other things the texts for *Andrea Chenier* and *Iris*. To follow up on their trying experience with the hugely successful book to *La Bohème* they would supply Puccini with the librettos for *Tosca* and *Madama Butterfly*. Illica was responsible for scenarios and outlines, while Giacosa wrote the verses, but as the work went on and on their separate functions, particularly on Illica's part, overlapped. The development of the text was troublesome; there were false starts, episodes and even a whole act discarded, and the proportionate participation of the various characters (particularly Schaunard) remained up in the air until late in 1895. Puccini's high-handed treatment of his librettists, his terse insistence upon revisions of passages already revised and re-revised, brought the fastidious Giacosa more than once to the point of wanting to throw over the whole project, and only the diplomacy of Ricordi kept the disaffected librettist to his task. One upshot of these troubles with the book was the loss to Puccini of the support of Boito, who had been instrumental in getting his first opera, *Le Villi*, produced in 1884, because Boito was a staunch friend of 'Pin' Giacosa and his whole family. By 1895 Boito had come to view Puccini as an intransigent boor who had insufficient respect for distinguished men of letters. Yet in the long view Puccini's sense of the theatre and of those novel effects that particularly suited his approach to operatic form has proved justified, if not his want of tact, for he and his collaborators were engaged upon creating something close to a new genre of opera.

In the light of the problems of completing the libretto, it is perhaps surprising that there are not more traces, such as the allusions to Mimi's Viscontino, to incidents that were discarded along the way. The text has much to commend it: much of the wording is felicitous for its wry wit or touching sentiment, the imagery is consistent and frequently apt and moving. The lines endow the sharply realized characters with sufficient poetic resonance often to raise them above their rather tawdry milieu. And if there are apparent inconsistencies in construction – for instance, Act Three ends with Mimi and Rodolfo deciding not to separate just yet, while Act Four begins with them in fact apart – Puccini understood how to minimize such problems with his gift for making the emotion of a moment credible and somehow stage-filling.

La Bohème occupies a special place in the Puccini canon. The fourth of his operas, it reveals a flexibility in the handling of musical ideas together with a praiseworthy economy that was contrary to his approach in the three earlier scores. His first attempt, *Le Villi*, shows Puccini rather awkwardly attempting to fuse traditional operatic and balletic elements into a coherent work; in addition for this score he supplied *entr'actes*, giving them what seems today the rather misleading and unoperatic designation of *Parte Sinfonica*, divided into a *Primo* and *Secondo Tempo*. Lengthy musical units are very much present in his second opera, the much-revised *Edgar*. That work was burdened with a far-fetched and cumbersome symbolic libretto, a misjudgement on Puccini's part that made him determined to avoid that pitfall at all costs in the future. In *Manon Lescaut*, Puccini had not yet attained to the aptness of proportion that is so remarkable in *La Bohème*, but it stands as an advance on its predecessors in etching more clearly individualized characters and in generating a more intense level of passionate utterance. Besides these improvements, however, the symphonic aspects of *Manon Lescaut*, particularly in Act One, were a consideration seized upon by the early critics such as George Bernard Shaw at the time of its London première in 1894. Notable as this tendency seemed at the time, the feature which with hindsight seems more important is the affirmation and clear focus upon what was to become Puccini's trademark – the tragedy of fragile sentiment. There had been moments of pathos, of course, in both *Le Villi* and *Edgar*, but these had been points of secondary rather than of primary importance.

The tragedy of fragile sentiment finds a more appropriate expression in *La Bohème* than in his earlier attempts largely because he had come to discover the value of understatement. He had learned how to let intimate, apparently casual, moments carry a full freight of significance. If the full-throated emotionalism exploited in *Manon Lescaut* seems at times over-italicized, over-emphatic, that failing can scarcely be ascribed to *La Bohème*. Puccini may have seemed to have turned over a new leaf with this opera, but there were, nevertheless, reassuring signs that he was a composer as adaptive and receptive to new modes of expression as could be desired, and also one with a readily identifiable individuality. The underlying consistency of his approach can be demonstrated by the easy absorption of self-borrowings of earlier music into the score of *La Bohème*. The opening music stems from his *Capriccio sinfonico* of 1883, the melody of Musetta's waltz comes from a *pièce d'occasion* composed to celebrate the launching of a battleship, while the Act Three quartet is adumbrated from a solo song, *Sole e amore*, which had appeared in a magazine back in 1888. Only a composer with a well-developed personal idiom could insert such disparate materials into new contexts where they seem inevitably to belong.

To account for the greater flexibility and economy of treatment that sets off *La Bohème* from Puccini's earlier operas, a benificent influence is not far to seek. Verdi's *Falstaff* had its première on February 9, 1893, just eight days after the first night of *Manon Lescaut*; it was the most newsworthy new opera of the day and it was making its initial rounds of the leading theatres just at the time Puccini was feeling his way into the composition of *La Bohème*. One aspect of Verdi's comedy that was invariably commented upon by its first reviewers was the mercurial pace of the action, the rapid succession of musical ideas presented and succeeded by others without being dilated upon in the traditional manner of *opera buffa*. The kaleidoscopic succession of musical ideas found in the humorous first halves of Acts One and Four of Puccini's opera demonstrates how Puccini adapted the rapid pace of *Falstaff* into his own idiom. In still another way an indebtedness to Verdi's practice in his final opera shows up in *La Bohème*. Such tonal descriptions, brief but instantly communicated, as the jingling coins in the purse that Ford offers Falstaff during their first encounter at the Garter Inn, provide an antecedent for Puccini's musical vignettes — Rodolfo tearing up his manuscript to feed the stove or flicking water on the face of the fainting Mimi. To say this is not to suggest that *La Bohème* is a direct imitation of *Falstaff*, but these references serve to point up the sponge-like ability of Puccini to absorb and digest influences, turning them to his own purposes.

If *La Bohème* is viewed against the panorama of Puccini's later operas, it will be seen to contain anticipations of them. For instance, the opening of Act Three that sets before us the snowy dawn at the Barrière d'Enfer distills a sense of time and weather which looks forward to the deceptively pastoral dawnscape introduction to the last act of *Tosca*. If Puccini was to go to considerable lengths in *Madama Butterfly* to evoke Japanese atmosphere and, later, in *Turandot* a Chinese ambience, by adapting authentic melodies into those scores, he had already made a partial step in that direction when he borrowed a scrap of French march music to accompany the soldiers that cross the stage near the end of Act Two of *La Bohème*. And yet there are details of this opera that proved so successful that Puccini did not choose (or dare) to repeat them. A single example may illustrate this point. Nothing could be more unobtrusive than Mimi's death, she slips away *pianissimo*, but how different the effect of Tosca's last defiant phrase with its top B flat as she leaps off the parapet, or the stressfulness of Butterfly's farewell to her little son, or (in *Suor Angelica*) the nagging guilt expressed by the bereft Angelica after she drinks the poisoned decoction, or even of the way the heretofore unobtrusive Liù (in *Turandot*) dominates the stage just before she dies. Never again would Puccini depict such a low-key death as Mimi's.

In *La Bohème*, it is ultimately the fine equilibrium of shifting moods, the strikingly economical transitions between them, that sets this opera apart from the rest of Puccini's output. In some respects *Il Tabarro* is his most thoroughly integrated score, for there every detail illuminates some aspect of the central triangle. Yet its over-riding sense of a barely-suppressed tension, which finally explodes, stands near the opposite end of a sliding scale from the deft development and release of dramatic pressure that animates *La Bohème*. In *Il Tabarro* an audience can understand the powerful emotions that assail Giorgetta, her lover Luigi, and her husband Michele, but that understanding does not move an audience in the way that *Bohème* does. The courageous humour, the pathetic details of futile gestures (like Musetta selling her earrings to buy Mimi a muff) and the moments of teasing charm, give an intimate comprehension of the characters and make *La Bohème* an endearing work.

In his later operas Puccini displays a mastery of more sophisticated techniques, but his mature resourcefulness was acquired at the cost of a certain spontaneity. The subject matter of *La Bohème* reminded Puccini of his carefree youthful days – he was 36 when he began composing it – and it enkindled in him a directness of communication coupled with an easy lightness of touch that he would never quite recapture.

Romance and Irony
A commentary on 'La Bohème'

Nicholas John

In a note prefacing their libretto for *La Bohème*, Giacosa and Illica declared that they had retained the right to treat the subject freely since Murger's book was 'perhaps the most free in modern literature'. The challenge was to adapt a book which caught the spirit of Bohemian life in a vivid series of unrelated incidents and characters. The result was a verse text with an elegantly symmetrical structure of four scenes and six principal characters. The three and a half years spent adjusting and revising the libretto (Illica began work on it in 1892) were exhausting for librettists, composer and publisher alike. Yet when Giacosa had once again threatened to resign because Puccini had asked him to rewrite some lines a fourth time, Ricordi played him some of the music, and he wrote with disarming honesty and perception:

> Puccini has surpassed all my expectations, and I now understand the reason for his tyranny over verses and accents. (July, 1895)

What, we may ask, attracted Puccini to this unusual and difficult source, and what were those expectations which he surpassed.

Alessandro Bonci as Rodolfo (Royal Opera House Archives)

Rosetta Pampanini as Mimì, a role which she performed at La Scala and Covent Garden around 1930.

Act Two in John Copley's production at Covent Garden with Marilyn Zschau as Musetta, Thomas Allen as Marcello, Neil Shicoff as Rodolfo, Ileana Cotrubas as Mimì, Gwynne Howell and Philip Gelling. (photo: Reg Wilson)

For a start, Puccini was originally considering another book: *La Lupa* (*The She-Wolf*) from the same set of stories by Giovanni Verga as Mascagni's triumphant first opera, *Cavalleria Rusticana* (1890). He only resolved not to pursue it after a research visit to Sicily in 1894. To Ricordi, he explained his reasons:

> ... the many dialogues in the libretto, which are drawn out to excessive lengths, and the unattractive characters, without a single luminous and appealing figure to stand out from them ...

Those telling adjectives — 'excessive', 'unattractive', 'luminous' — hint at the qualities he found in *La Bohème*. He resolved to wait for *La Lupa*'s success as a stage play before picking up the subject again. Although Murger's book had been a great success as a play, the stage version is very different from Puccini's libretto. It resembles in some respects the play which Dumas the Younger had adapted from his best-selling novel about *The Lady of the Camellias* in 1849 — another portrait drawn from contemporary Parisian life which had to be sentimentalised for presentation on the stage. The play centres around the efforts of Rodolfo's wealthy uncle (who is mentioned in the opera only as a future source of prosperity) to marry off his nephew to a rich widow. He resorts to forged letters to prove Mimi is faithless and when he relents, as in *La Dame aux Camélias*, he is too late. Yet however much the success of this stage version convinced Puccini that the subject had dramatic potential, *La Bohème* is inspired by the book rather than the play, and in this differs from Puccini's other great operas.

Just how difficult it was to evolve a balanced libretto out of the book is illustrated by the weaknesses of Leoncavallo's text for his opera on the same subject. The simultaneous public announcements of these two operas in Milan in March 1893 led to fierce recriminations and a spirit of competition to which Puccini reacted by saying 'let the public judge'. That Leoncavallo only completed his opera in 1898 suggests that he was not as far advanced in 1893 as he made out — but the fact remains that Puccini was always drawn to a subject once it had been chosen by someone else. His success with *Manon Lescaut* (1893) followed Massenet's opera (1884) and his next choice (*Tosca*) was only determined finally when he heard that Franchetti had decided to work on it.

Murger's book attracted Puccini not so much by a plot as some strong situations. In July 1894, he described to Ricordi how vividly he imagined each scene:

> I have my conception of *Bohème* but with the *Latin Quarter* ... Musetta's scene, which was my idea. I want the death [of Mimi] as I had imagined it, and I shall be sure then of writing a vital and original work. As to the *Barrière* ... I wanted a canvas that would allow me to spread myself a little more lyrically ...

Situations which move audiences, whether to tears or to laughter, and without 'excessive dialogue' form the kernels of the acts of Puccini's opera. Aware of this, his librettists called them not Acts but *'Quadri'*, that is *'Tableaux'*, or even *'Impressions'*. Their libretto was devised as a balanced dramatic sequence around these crucial scenes. In the course of this construction process, as late as December 1893, an entire act, which was to follow the *Barrière d'Enfer*, was discarded although it had already been versified. It involved a party thrown by Musetta in the courtyard of her house while her furniture was being removed by the bailiffs. A similar scene in Leoncavallo's opera demonstrates how this tips the balance of interest in favour of the flamboyant characters of Marcello and Musetta. It would also have repeated the high-spirited atmosphere of the 'Momus' Act, and cutting redundant material to maximise effect was a canon in Puccini's ideas about drama.

In addition, there was a risk that this scene might make Mimi, that 'single luminous character' Puccini so much cherished, appear unsympathetic. It showed her flirting with a rich student, the Viscontino Paolo, and arousing Rodolfo's furious jealousy. It has to be admitted that the cut has left some inconsistencies in the action and an ambiguity about her character. Each interpreter of the role must now decide how far she is the devoted and hard-working heroine of sentimental drama, or an amalgam of the various temperamental and frivolous girls in Murger's book. A delightful sense of humour, at any rate, is present in many of her scenes in the opera. 'She is merry and smiling' protests Rodolfo in Act Three, even though she is fatally ill. And in the light of this resilience, her bewildered appeal to Marcello is doubly sympathetic.

The work of synchronising the text and the music progressed with painful slowness. Puccini did not even set all the lines that his librettists eventually published as the libretto. On occasion, he wanted 'a little more air' — as in the 'Momus' Act, after he had seen it staged in Turin — and he frequently conceived musical motifs in such detail that the words had to be supplied to fit the metre. A celebrated example, also from the Second Act, is Musetta's waltz for which Giacosa was invited to write poetry to match *'Coccoricó, coccoricó, bistécca'* (literally: 'Cock-adoodle-do, cock-adoodle-do, beefsteak). The result was *'Quando m'en vo, quando m'en vo soletta'* ('As through the street, as through the street I wander'). None of this, however, detracts from the vital element which the librettists contributed. Their four 'tableaux' are indeed scarcely related by plot. Yet Illica's dramatic structure gives this opera about Bohemian life a formal balance, and the imagery of Giacosa's poetry illustrates and underlines its emotional crises. A unity of conception radiates

Benoit calls for the rent in the wartime touring production by Tyrone Guthrie for Sadler's Wells. (photo: Michael Boys)

through the poetry from the vivid situations which are the heart of the opera. Thus, as William Ashbrook has noted[*] it is the idea of cold which most closely unifies the opera. In the first three acts a different atmosphere is carefully evoked: the freezing garret, the hilarity and bustle of the street on Christmas Eve, the miserably snowy February dawn. In these Acts the dream of Springtime, of sunlight and flowers, of warmth and perfumes, recurs as the natural image of love. But when Spring comes, in the Fourth Act, the irony is that it brings desolation: the ray of sunshine strikes Mimi's death-bed.

The many facets of irony and contrast are, in fact, the key to the spirit of *La Bohème*. One aspect is, of course, the outlook on life of the Bohemians themselves. Poking fun at pretentiousness and pomposity involves mimicry and mock solemnity. In the opening scene, for instance, Rodolfo's melodrama is burnt with hilarious formality, each of its five acts receiving the grave consideration it never got on stage . . . but the fire dies out . . . there is a tragic pause . . . and in an explosion of mirth, his friends cry 'Down with the author!' Then Schaunard's monologue detailing the way he was commissioned to kill a parrot by playing the violin ends tragically with the words *'da Socrate morì'* ('as Socrates he died'). 'Who?' asks Colline and the furiously energetic 2/4 motif starts up again. And the reception of Benoit with exaggerated courtesy culminates in a quite disproportionate burst of mock indignation.

By contrast with these (and many more) examples of ironic gravity, there is a touchingly sincere formality about Mimi's behaviour and their conduct towards her. Musetta's flamboyance is a foil for her, and the two affairs are very delicately contrasted to show the tenderness of the love of Mimi and Rodolfo. Puccini develops this very consistently. He dwells upon the little sentences of her first appearance repeating the rather formal *staccato* phrase (*andante moderato, pianissimo*) which accompanies them five times before she

[*] *The Operas of Puccini* (Cassell, 1969)

says good night. Then he repeats her apologies for disturbing Rodolfo. We may guess, of course, that her adventure has been partly thought out in advance and that she is not being entirely spontaneous — somehow the music flows just too smoothly from the unresolved chord before *'Buona sera'* to *'Oh sventata!'* The libretto nevertheless expressly notes that it is not the girl — as it was in Murger's tale — but the boy who slips the key into his pocket, although she guesses what has happened. Finally, the overall pattern of the two arias (in themselves perfectly balanced), in which they introduce themselves, and the briefly ecstatic duet, in which they fall in love, is underlined by the return of the opening motif [8] at the close of the Act.

Formality is stressed again when Rodolfo presents Mimi to his friends as *'La Poesia'*, his 'Inspiration'. 'Heavens what lofty sentiments!' exclaims Marcello, while the others drop Latin tags; but he then very delicately invites her (*'Signorina Mimi'*) to tell them what Rodolfo has bought her. We can sense Mimi rising to the occasion in her reply. Obviously, her 'Farewell' in Act Three and her gentle greetings and reminiscences in the final act maintain this sweet formality which, in its restraint, can suggest both fragility and deep emotion.

The result of the libretto's persistent use of irony is to throw the truly felt emotions of the subject into relief. It gives a sense of actuality not only to the death of Mimi but to the moments when the emotion overflows, and Puccini captures every gradation between irony and idealism in a score of exceptional orchestral and melodic inspiration. Central to any discussion of the sense of formality in this opera about the Bohemian spirit is its sophisticated musical structure analysed by Edward Greenfield in the next essay. It is appropriate here to mention just three points.

Puccini's use of silence is remarkable. There is a pause before each aria or important ensemble to mark it apart from the surrounding musical texture. But many dramatic or amusing phrases stick in the mind because he also has a habit of suddenly allowing a voice to sound, unaccompanied or barely supported. This is particularly well illustrated by the Second Act in which the interjections ('Parpignol!' 'Want a trumpet, want a drum!' 'What will all the people say?' 'I must get rid of the old boy!' 'We have come to the last act') make us aware of Puccini's control and of the theatricality of the scene. The score also features pauses for a hundred other effects — expectation, for instance, or insinuation, or sheer dramatic tension.

As notable as the sudden silences are the score's fine dynamics. Ricordi exclaimed at:

> . . . all kinds of possible and impossible indications. It is a forest of *p-pp-ppp*, of *f-ff-fff-ffff*, of slowing up and of going ahead, so that the conductors will lose their heads.

Puccini replied:

> . . . As for the *pp*s and the *ff*s of the score, if I have overdone them it is because, *as Verdi says*, when one wants *piano* one puts *ppp*.

They are vital to *La Bohème*, an opera in which the infinitely subtle changes in volume, orchestral colour and tempo suggest the depth and the transience of youthful emotions. If Puccini avoided the rancid unpleasantness of poverty which underlies the impact of Murger's book, he was astonishingly sensitive to the spontaneity and intensity of the characters' emotions. The gaiety and emotionalism has at times a feverish quality that reminds us that Mimi is consumptive, Schaunard smokes 'hatchisch' (according to Murger) and that all of them are doomed to early death. There is evidence enough in the text of

Puccini's delight in word games and puns, and in the score he enjoys every opportunity to add vivid orchestral comments — the curious noise when Schaunard imitates the English 'milord' is a memorable but minute instance. This attention to comic detail for effect reaches a climax in the Bohemians' scenes in the first and last acts.

Lastly, his treatment of musical themes in *La Bohème* is peculiarly successful because dreams and recollections are so central to the opera. Puccini was well aware of this when he reintroduced the motifs of the First Act in the final scene. He further bound the score together with a number of themes that resemble one another in that they move note by note up and down a scale [3, 5, 8, 9, 11, 12, etc.]. As a result any wider vocal leaps are immediately distinctive and, since Mimi's part contains many such phrases, her character — and references to her, and to love and Springtime — are clearly defined and associated. They also emphasise those almost self-consciously poetic moments such as Rodolfo's declaration of love, or Mimi's Farewell, and display Musetta's histrionic tantrums.

In short, Puccini's muse was exactly suited to this mixture of heightened emotion and comic chatter. In just the sense that the Bohemians are aware that they over-react to life, and enjoy doing so, Puccini counterpoints the consciously melodramatic response of his glorious melodies with ironic and comic declamation. The Bohemians dream of poetry and infinite wealth — not of saving enough money to have a secure living, or of naughty nights on the town, like their landlord, Benoit. Puccini's music has such overwhelming emotional appeal because the composer sets it so firmly in perspective. He has the power to express the sheer joy of falling in love because every expressive effect is minutely calculated within the formal patterns that make us laugh as well as cry.

Benoit describes his exploits in the 1977 ENO production: Christian du Plessis, Eric Shilling, John Tomlinson, David Rendall and David Marsh. (photo: Andrew March)

Act One In the Attic

The pace and spirit of the Bohemians' gossip and tomfoolery is immediately established by [1]. Puccini's lyrical vein transforms even the energetic declamation of the opening lines. Their vivacious wit is typical of the excellent turns of phrase, rich vocabulary, Classical and literary references, puns and aphorisms throughout the opera. Although Puccini is not too particular about the association of motif [1] with the Bohemians, or even with life in the attic, and Marcello, the painter, alone of the principals has no motif of his own, theme [2] is consistently identified with Rodolfo, the poet. In *'Nei cieli bigi'* ('Look how the smoke . . .') Rodolfo energetically complains that their stove, unlike all the others in Paris, makes no smoke and hits upon the idea of using his play — a five-act melodrama — as fuel. A third Bohemian, the philosopher Colline, joins them [3] to applaud the work's success — as it is received by the fire. A change of key and rhythm announces the arrival of the fourth Bohemian, the musician Schaunard, with some unexpected money and provisions [4]. They ignore him (because they are ravenous) as he describes his adventure, and Puccini orchestrates each twist of the story with obsessive care. Another sudden pause highlights the death of the parrot he was paid to kill: realising they have not been listening he upbraids them for eating at home when the Latin Quarter [13, 14] would welcome them . . . The fast ensemble is cut short by the arrival of their landlord; in a sudden pause, his knocks are heard at the door. A change of key and rhythm smoothly depict the insinuating way the Bohemians operate to loosen his tongue and remove from his pockets the rent they have just paid him. Another change of key announces their indignation that he should be unfaithful to his wife . . . and a phoney moral chorus speeds him on his way. Three of the Bohemians follow him, leaving Rodolfo alone to finish writing. Thus the scene progresses in comic reversals and triumphant solutions. In ten minutes, much of the thematic material of the opera has already been introduced. A sudden hush descends and the strings softly (*ppp*) announce the timid appearance of Mimi, their neighbour. Puccini paces their tentative conversation with precise care for each move and gesture; the vocal phrases are scarcely accompanied: just a single example *'Che bella bambina'* ('So young and so lovely') has unforgettable resonance.

Rodolfo's aria, *'Che gelida manina'* ('Your tiny hand is frozen') follows a simple pattern: [8a, 6a], some declamatory self-interrogation and then his opening theme [2] is followed by [9]. He tells Mimi that her eyes have stolen all his dreams from him. As an indication of the subtlety and sensitivity of Puccini's dynamics the orchestral accompaniment moves from *forte con anima* in one bar through a two bar *crescendo* and *diminuendo* to end *ppp*. Only after the 1896 Turin performances did Puccini settle the opening key of the aria in D♭. Rodolfo's self-portrait is eloquent, as befits a poet and a dreamer. For all his impracticality he shares with Cavaradossi, Puccini's other artist hero (in *Tosca*), a lively taste for romance and for sensual love.

Mimi repeats the falling cadences of his last phrases. She too is a dreamer and the many echoes in her reply of the structure and melodic phrases of his aria create a magical sense of intimacy. She begins with two statements of [10], followed by [11]; a restatement of [10] and then [12] twice, an expansion to describe the arrival of Spring which parallels the climax [9] of Rodolfo's aria, and a return to [11]; she ends with little sentences to be 'sung naturally without a strict tempo'. The aria moves from the unaccompanied *'Vivo sola, soletta'* ('I'm alone but not lonely') through an expansive evocation of the Spring sunshine to the wistful recollection that the flowers she embroiders have no scent. Puccini marks this image of flowers without perfume — the symbol of life without love — by a grace note and low strings.

Giacomo Aragall and Ileana Cotrubas at Covent Garden in 1979 (photo: Clive Barda)

The Bohemians interrupt from outside in a chorus that could not be more of a contrast. Yet Marcello's receding voice blends wonderfully with Rodolfo's when he turns to see Mimi 'as if wreathed in moonlight'. The first ecstasy of mutual love is expressed in the single bar where Puccini asks the full orchestra to play *fff largamente sostenuto* and *with emotion*. The duet rapidly diminishes to *piano espressivo*. By silence in the orchestra, Puccini is able to accentuate without undue emphasis Rodolfo's question as to what will happen when they return from Momus. Her arch reply *'Curioso'* ('Who knows sir?') has an ambiguous modesty. The Act ends, as their meeting began, with courtesies exchanged and the theme [8] repeated in the orchestra. Their voices fade away off-stage, the strings supporting and continuing Mimi's high C even more quietly.

Act Two In the Latin Quarter

Christmas Eve in Paris is still a lively night to eat out, do last minute shopping and gather to go to Midnight Mass. The Café Momus — appropriately named after Momos, the Greek God of raillery and sarcasm — was a very fashionable restaurant. The Bohemians are pictured not so much against the background of the milling crowds, as actually part of them. A comparison with the Cours-la-Reine scene in Massenet's *Manon* (1884) shows its special quality, since both involve similarly complex scenes of choruses (with authentic street cries) and short but important exchanges for the principal characters. Where the French composer leaves the ensembles, recitatives and solo numbers in relatively distinct sections, the Italian weaves the fragments of vocal lines into a much closer texture. It makes for amusing and illuminating juxtapositions: Marcello, offering his heart for sale, imitates the shouts of the food sellers; Mimì's acquisitive instincts and roving eye are surely meant to be compared to the children's intense but innocent excitement when the toyseller arrives. None of this came easily. Giacosa wrote to Ricordi in October 1893:

> [It] presented me with an insuperable difficulty. I do not feel it: I am not inside it, I do not succeed in creating that illusion, that imaginary reality, without which nothing can be achieved. For those few scenes I have wasted more paper and racked my brain more than I have for any of my own plays.

The way Puccini shifts attention from the tumultuous crowd to individual voices gives a theatrical, we might say cinematic, feel to the scene, as though general camera shots are interspersed with close-ups. The device is entirely appropriate to suggest the brilliantly-lit Parisian street scene, where the lamps

Christian du Plessis (Marcello), Lorna Haywood (Musetta) and Denis Dowling (Alcindoro) in the 1977 ENO production (photo: John Garner)

Marie Collier as Musetta at Covent Garden in 1961. (Royal Opera House Archives)

A design for Musetta by Connelli, 1899 (Royal Opera House Archives)

make an artificial daylight and cast dramatically dark shadows. As before, the changes of tempo and key spotlight each incident, and sudden silences broken only by a single voice make details vivid, and accentuate the size and sound of the ensembles. The formality and lyricism of the Bohemians' supper interlude is interrupted by Musetta's entrance [15]. Her ostentatious vocal leaps, heard in parts of [15] and [16], attract attention and Marcello's music is marked with emphasis and bitterness, as the ingenious duet, in which they sing against rather than with one another, rises to a climax. This, added to the already complex musical texture, throws the sudden pause (with three *staccato* harp notes) and Musetta's slow waltz into high relief. The Gavotte Massenet wrote for Manon in Cours-la-Reine is also an exquisite display of seductive, sophisticated charm but serves no direct dramatic purpose. Musetta's Waltz, on the other hand, gains immeasurably from the context: it overwhelms Marcello, infuriates Alcindoro, impresses Mimi enormously — and finally flows without a break for applause back into the ensemble.* In the opening act of Murger's play, Musetta shows her ankles as she climbs over a wall and, in a subsequent scene, avoids paying rent by allowing Benoit to tie up her shoe. The opera amalgamates these episodes and successfully establishes her coquettish yet sympathetic character as a foil to Mimi. Indeed the languorous beauty of her waltz perfectly conveys her histrionic talents and truly appealing charm. The role is, nevertheless, a difficult one to encompass vocally, because it requires both light coloratura and lyrical expressiveness.

* According to *200 Years of Opera at Covent Garden* (Harold Rosenthal), Ljuba Welitsch in 1949 stopped the show for several minutes with her sensational rendering, to the objections of the 'more austere' critics and the delight of the audience.

The introduction of an authentic 1830s French march [18] for a stage band of piccolos, trumpets and drums is yet another diversion. The tension of the rhythms (2/4 against 3/4) immediately catches the atmosphere of general anticipation — and of not being able to pay the Momus bill. By the time the full orchestra takes over, Musetta has resolved the problem by leaving it for Alcindoro, and not a cloud is left in the unison chorus that brings the curtain down.

This conclusion was only conceived after the 1896 Turin première: Puccini complained that the original conclusion in which Alcindoro had some lines to speak after the Bohemians and the band had left in a chorus of gaiety, was a 'ghiaccio' — rather a chilling anticlimax. The final reprise of the Tattoo, with Musetta borne aloft by the crowd, and Alcindoro's comic but mimed return, keeps the high spirits at a peak.

Act Three The Barrière d'Enfer

With hollow fifths descending slowly and *pianissimo* [19], the opening theme echoes the boisterous motif [13] which announced Christmas Eve in the Latin Quarter. It is a cold, miserable February dawn. Perhaps his obsession with duck-shooting gave Puccini a special affinity with the hushed grey hour before dawn when hunters slip out into the rushes to wait for game. We need only think of the shepherd boy and the matin bells of Rome in the Third Act of *Tosca* when Cavaradossi awaits execution; or the *entr'acte* between the Second and Third Acts of *Madama Butterfly* when Butterfly stays up waiting for her husband in vain and the 'humming chorus' from the harbour announces a new day; or, indeed, the climax of *Turandot* when the dawn after the sleepless night of tragedy finally melts the ice-cold heart of the Princess with love, to notice his predilection for the special qualities of this twilight hour.

As he did with the street cries and Tattoo band of the previous act, Puccini fits ordinary sounds from the stage — milk-sellers' cries, cracking whips, donkey-cart bells, church bells — into the orchestral sound. The dreamy evocation of 'Paris awakes' in Charpentier's *Louise* (1900) is another sound picture of the city, actually inspired by the street life outside the composer's Montmartre studio:

> After a night of hard labour, when the blue light of dawn touched my paper, the street cries seemed to me like smiling greetings from friends who wished my work well, in the knowledge that I was trying to write their story, and wanted to encourage me.

The precise and matter-of-fact exchanges in Puccini's score, however, offset rather than reflect the emotional turmoil of the Bohemians.

The Act is built around the ironic contrast of the two relationships. Mimi and Rodolfo have separately come to ask Marcello for help in sorting out their problems. The heightened emotionalism of the situation is naturally melodramatic and we, perhaps, like Marcello, do not quite believe all they say. When Mimi complains that Rodolfo is insanely jealous [21], we may suspect that he might have had a reason. The libretto, from which the scene in Musetta's courtyard was cut, now refers ambiguously to the flirtatious side of her character which was so clear in the book, but eliminated in the play. The musical phrases are repeated higher and higher as she becomes more passionate, and the orchestra gives the sudden breaks in the pointed vocal line full effect with ominous bass chords. At the climax — a single *fortissimo* bass chord — Mimi drops to a monotone (*declamato*) as though her energy is really spent. Puccini continuously punctuates the outbursts of melody with the

Voytek's design for the 1962 Sadler's Wells production.

simplest of phrases. This increases the tension and suggests the characters are not unselfconscious of the scenes they are making. By way of reply, Marcello describes his life with Musetta as 'laughter, music and song — the flowers of love' and taking up Mimi's vocal line in sympathy, suggests that she should leave Rodolfo.

For his part, Rodolfo moves from uncharacteristic decisiveness, to a show of nervous irritation [22], to futile protestations and, finally, deeply moving despair. To a funereal (*lento triste*) motif [23], he declares that Mimi needs 'more than love' to save her life. The three voices are drawn inexorably together and a trio develops: Mimi stunned and despairing, Rodolfo protesting against the injustice of an abrupt separation, Marcello frustrated at being unable to help. The cough [6, 24] which played such an important part in bringing Mimi and Rodolfo together now reveals her presence; simultaneously, Musetta's brazen laughter [16] distracts Marcello's attention. Perhaps more than Rodolfo, he knows what jealousy means; certainly the reunion of Rodolfo and Mimi is all the more touching because his jealousy was actually motivated by self-denial. The sweet formality and restraint of Mimi's farewell — to life and love together — powerfully contrast with Rodolfo's impassioned outbursts. Her mood of graceful resignation is, of course, calculated to make Rodolfo's decision to separate unbearable. The themes [10, 12b, 11] associated with their happiness are recalled one by one: Rodolfo is overwhelmed by nostalgia. She teases his too-rosy memories ('Farewell to jealousy and anger . . .' [26]) and their voices soar together in a long lyrical melody [27] apparently oblivious of the sound of smashing plates and raised angry voices (all *staccato* leaps and semiquavers). A hugely comic effect is achieved by the way particularly vituperative insults and sarcastic courtesies shatter the pauses between the lovers' phrases. At almost every bar the tempo and dynamics are adjusted for a perfect counterpoint of the quartet: we are swept along on a surge of emotion, aware that the reunion may be as temporary as the suddenness of the quarrel. Puccini repeats the harmonious close of the First Act, allowing the voices to drift away off-stage. But he frames his picture of quarrels and reconciliations with the sharp, loud chord (*fff*) that opened the Act, perhaps suggesting that any dream of Spring will be cut short.

Act Four In the Attic

The last tableau of the opera is set, like the first, in the Bohemians' attic. Although it is only just Spring, Mimi and Rodolfo are apart — we learn that she has been living with the Viscontino, whose appearance in Musetta's Courtyard Scene was cut. Reminiscences of earlier happiness stop Rodolfo and Marcello from working. Their duet is based like so many of the melodies in *La Bohème* on a gradually rising and falling theme [28]. Its sentimentality is amusingly broken by Rodolfo's question *'Che ora sia?'* ('What is the time now?') and the quickening tempo of their friends' return. Whatever other autobiographical elements there may be in Puccini's opera, these moments when the artists find they have no inspiration and they begin to day-dream have the clearest ring of truth. Similarly, it is the Puccini who enjoyed the company of gossiping, card-playing intimate friends in the *Club la Bohème* (one rule was: 'Silence is forbidden') who could catch the spirit of the Bohemians' energetic tomfoolery. In Act One, Mimi's timid entry at a quiet moment in the score began the second part of the scene; in this Act Musetta's arrival interrupts the height of the gaiety — so it was vital that this should be sufficiently high-spirited for the interruption to be fully effective. For this purpose the scene originally included a mock solemn toast which caused enormous problems, mainly because Giacosa had given each character verses in a different metre. Puccini finally discarded it in favour of the three shouts of 'No!' when Schaunard proposes to give a high flown speech! The quick changes of tempo, key and melody are brought to a frenetic climax when the

The last scene in the 1977 ENO production with Robert Ferguson and Josephine Barstow (photo: John Garner)

25

different rhythms of gavotte, fandango and quadrille are proposed, and Colline and Schaunard work off excess energy in a mock duel (*allegro spigliato*).

The tension of the final scene is conveyed by the monotonous, almost spoken, vocal lines which suggest both Mimi's weakness and the others' anxious whispers. The orchestral reminiscences point touching ironies: when Musetta describes Mimi's wish to die near Rodolfo, the delicate trills associated with the dream of Spring are heard. In the crisis, Musetta's practicality shows its value and her genuine attachment to Mimi is movingly suggested. Among the general points to show her thoughtfulness, it is nice to see how Puccini makes her break off from praying to tell Marcello to shade Mimi's face from the light of the spirit lamp.

Puccini's ability to breathe life into inanimate objects is well known. Insofar as they have special significance for the characters they become powerful symbols for the audience (Tosca's fan, Butterfly's sword spring immediately to mind, not to mention the lists of little belongings in which both Mimi and Butterfly are lovingly indulged). Here, the things they had on Christmas Eve are recalled — Mimi's bonnet, Musetta's muff — along with remembered happiness. In a daring use of irony, Puccini conceived a grandly tragic aria for Colline to sing to the long-coat he bought that evening: the powerful impact of the music involves our emotions to a much greater extent than is actually warranted by the more or less futile gesture. Puccini forces us to smile at our susceptibility to tears; and that smile prepares a sense of the inescapable and tragic reality of the death of Mimi.

Her last duet with Rodolfo has many touches of gaiety to highlight her passionate sincerity [31]. The fragility of their music — the reminiscence of 'Mi chiamano Mimì' [10], for instance, is extenuated over twice its original length — is emphasised by the emptiness of the scoring and persistent strings in the bass. In the autograph score, Puccini marked the chord where Mimi dies *pppppppp* and drew a skull and cross-bones beside it. The loud repeat of the theme of the last duet [31] fades away to *pp*, and the opera finishes, ironically enough, with the chords that end Colline's lament. Puccini later said that, when he had completed this scene, he 'had to get up and, standing in the middle of the study, alone in the silence of the night, I began to weep like a child. It was as though I had seen my own child die'.

This last act alone remained the one he preferred to hear.

The death of Mimì at La Scala in the 1963 production (Teatro alla Scala)

The Music of 'La Bohème'

Edward Greenfield

La Bohème has long been a victim of its own popularity. Even among Puccini's operas it is recognisably the easiest of all to assimilate. This was the opera which two successive British monarchs, Edward VII and George V — neither much given to music-loving and as different from one another as father and son can be — both counted their favourite in the whole repertory, for them a very modern work. It is as near an unsinkable opera as we have — proof against the least inspired singing, the roughest playing and musical direction — yet its very accessibility tends to obscure the musical genius behind the score.

La Bohème is a great opera not simply because it illustrates big open emotions with music that is easy to listen to, tuneful on the one hand, atmospheric on the other, but because the purely musical argument has a concentration and consistency to rival that of works — not just operas — of far more ambitious intellectual pretensions. So skilfully does Puccini conceal his consummate technique, that one can easily fail to appreciate even the finesse of the orchestration, its remarkable restraint even at climaxes, let alone the cohesion of the overall structure, or the niceties of melodic consistency. The tunes of *La Bohème* are not just immediately memorable, they hang together in a way that can be readily analysed. To enjoy *La Bohème* one does not necessarily have to appreciate how cunning the composer is in this way, but musical analysis helps to explain why the opera — which early commentators so readily dismissed (see page 7) — remains so satisfying after so much repetition.

The very opening of *La Bohème* gives a clue to an aspect of the work not often appreciated. The theme of the Bohemians at the very start [1] was taken from Puccini's early *Capriccio sinfonico*, fair indication that it was not just a question for him of setting a jolly mood for Bohemians' highjinks, but of commanding attention musically in a way that a symphonic work does. Not only that, Puccini follows up the exposition of that striking theme with another that provides a contrast closely akin to that of a symphonic second subject, Rodolfo's first theme on *'Nei cieli bigi . . .'* (*'Look how the smoke . . .'*) [2]. Pursuing the sonata-form parallel, one can point to such a moment as the pause (before Fig. 10 in the score) on the harp cadence which precedes the arrival of Schaunard's wine and cigars as being very like the end of a symphonic exposition section. *Manon Lescaut* before *La Bohème*, and *Tosca* immediately following, provide exactly parallel moments, to suggest that it was an effect which Puccini consciously nurtured.

It would be too much to deduce that Puccini thought of Act One of *La Bohème* as a sonata-form structure, but these specific pointers go along with an overall shape for the whole opera which itself is akin to that of a four-movement symphony. Act Four like Act One uses that *Capriccio sinfonico* theme prominently to suggest a finale, parallel to the first movement. Act Two, shorter than the others, brisk and colourful, is comparably established as the *scherzo* of the work, while Act Three in which chill scene-setting is followed by lyrical outpouring, takes on the function of a slow movement. That balance is the more clearly appreciated on the gramophone, where without

Mirella Freni as Mimì (Teatro alla Scala) *Nellie Melba as Mimì (Royal Opera House Archives)*

intervals one can readily compare the cohesion of the four 'movements' with that of a Mahler symphony of roughly comparable length.

That symphonic impression is enhanced by the directness and economy with which Puccini established mood and atmosphere. The outer acts have their striking opening in the *Capriccio sinfonico* theme, but Acts Two and Three are equally memorable in their immediate impact at the rise of the curtain, both effectively illustrating another quality of Puccini as musician, his magpie ability to adopt a technique and make it totally his. The brightness and colour of the opening of the Second Act, with three trumpets playing parallel chords *Allegro focoso* [13], is in itself so immediately colourful and attractive, anticipating similar effects in Stravinsky's *Petrushka* by some 15 years, that one is liable to forget just how original that idea is, when related to the time of composition in the mid-1890s. Puccini was not only a lover of French music, he liked to keep abreast of the latest developments among his contemporaries, and one can only marvel that the parallel chord technique which at the time Debussy was only just developing could here have such a different impact, sharp and bright, not misty at all. Yet look at the flutes and harp in prinking parallel fifths [19] over tremolo cellos *pianissimo* at the opening of the Third Act, where Puccini seems directly to be taking on the French Impressionists at their own game. The further marvel is that in a very Puccinian way the parallel chords in Act Two and fifths in Act Three have an obvious musical kinship even while their atmospheric effect could hardly be more sharply contrasted, the one bright and electrifying, the other chill and grey, the simplest possible illustration of dawn at the Barrière d'Enfer. And as though the initial chill is not intense enough, it is made even keener by his favourite trick of offstage voices, by the waiting market people's cries outside the gate and more particularly by the snatches of jolly singing inside the inn, suggesting warmth to be envied. And how cleverly Puccini uses the simple device of a perfect cadence, *fortissimo*, from the full orchestra to punctuate the sustained *pianissimo*, later using it to provide a final pay-off to the Act, when Mimi and Rodolfo's duet fades away offstage and the cadence then snaps the curtain shut. The parallel is clear between that curtain and the end of Act One, where similarly Mimi and Rodolfo depart in offstage duet but where the undisturbed *diminuendo* leaves us to our dreams. It is such balancing of effect that significantly reinforces Puccini's musical cohesion.

Although today Puccini must almost inevitably appear as a musical conservative, particularly in the case of a score that was easily accessible even for early audiences (contrast the situation today with new operas); it has to be emphasised how shrewdly he used new techniques. In Act One where he illustrates the burning of Rodolfo's manuscript with more parallel chords he lays them out to imply bitonality, the common chord of G flat major against the chord of E flat minor. And if in 1896 it could hardly be regarded as revolutionary to take a Wagnerian stance with leit-motifs woven together in thematic representation, that profound debt tends to be overlooked. If in *Manon Lescaut* ill-digested Wagnerian passages may be detected, the symphonic *intermezzo* before the Third Act sounding like an Italian *Tristan*, *La Bohème* shows the influence completely assimilated. One might argue that the conversational speed of the Bohemians' music in *La Bohème* owes far more to the immediate example of Verdi's *Falstaff*, first heard in 1893 three years before *La Bohème*. Clearly Puccini drew on that source, but in the light of the symphonic shaping of the whole score, the interplay of often fragmentary melodic patterns can in effect be regarded as 'development texture', not unlike the developmental patterning which in Wagner is always counted symphonic.

If many of Puccini's contemporaries were trying to get the best of both worlds, writing through-composed operas which yet had the immediate popular appeal of earlier Italian models with their set numbers, he was perhaps the most successful of all in presenting his arias and ensembles fully and powerfully, and not merely as cherries on the cake. His success lay fundamentally in his genius as a melodist, which allowed him to present even within a generally melodic texture passages of heightened melody guaranteed to catch in the memory. Dr Mosco Carner and others have analysed how Puccini's melodies acquire their distinctive character from typical tune-shapes, such as the rising scale or the falling wide interval of a fourth or fifth, but if analysis were enough, imitators would be able to write at will melodies just as memorable, which manifestly is not so. Puccini's close contemporaries were generally less successful than he in the use of heightened melody for salient arias and ensembles — think of Giordano in *Andrea Chenier* or of Leoncavallo after *I pagliacci* — and nowhere is his success more assured than in *La Bohème*.

Given that success, demonstrating Puccini as one of Western music's supreme melodists, it is fascinating to discover that analysis of those big melodies in *La Bohème* suggests a coordination which is not often appreciated, yet helps to explain the opera's consistency. It is not just a question of Puccini's use of leit-motifs, far less intensive than in Wagner, but of patterning within the melodies, particularly striking in the incomparable sequence of three set numbers which ends Act One — Rodolfo's aria *Che gelida manina'*, ('Your tiny hand is frozen'), Mimi's aria *'Sì, mi chiamano Mimì'* (I'm always called Mimi') and their duet *'O soave fanciulla'* ('Lovely maid in the

Dora Labette, the English concert artist who sang as 'an outstanding but unknown Italian soprano, Lisa Perli' at Covent Garden in 1935 with Heddle Nash as Rodolfo. According to Harold Rosenthal, Sir Thomas Beecham said he was unaware of the deception which was revealed in the press the day after the première. (Royal Opera House Archives)

moonlight'). It is evident enough that the melody of the first part of *'Che gelida manina'* is firmly based on the Rodolfo theme *'Nei cieli bigi'* [2], the original 6/8 gallumphing transformed into passionate soaring for the beloved. It is an obvious point of balance too that the duet which brings the lovers together develops the main theme of Rodolfo's aria, *'Talor dal mio forziere'* ('Two lovely eyes have stolen') [9]. Significantly the melody of the duet may be

Rodolfo's, but the key is surely Mimi's — A major just one degree from the equivocal D major with which Puccini introduces *'Sì, mi chiamano Mimi'* slightly uncertain, brittle after the warmth of Rodolfo's A flat aria. Far subtler are the balances not immediately noticeable. So the tune of *'Talor dal mio forziere'* [9] has already been hinted at in the *Andantino mosso* section of the Benoit episode earlier in Act One.

What is more surprising is the family likeness that can be found between that big tune and the main melody of Mimi's aria [11]. The outline of Mimi's phrase on *'Mi piaccion quelle cose'* ('These flowers give me pleasure') is remarkably similar except that it curves up instead of down at the end, and paradoxically the likeness would no doubt have been noted more readily had the tunes themselves not become so familiar. Another likeness between the two arias lies in Puccini's persistent use of feminine endings to phrases, snapping down in wide intervals from accented notes, usually at the beginning of the bar. So in Mimi's aria that specific fingerprint comes on the words *'Lucia'* (her name), *'rose'*, *'primavere'*, and at the end of the aria's climactic phrase on *'fior'*, where earlier in *'Che gelida manina'* the words so emphasised on salient dropping fifths are *'Sogni miei'*, *'Occhi belli'* and *'La Speranza'*. If there is obvious consistency between 'rose', 'spring', 'flower' and the name of the heroine, so clearly Rodolfo's references to 'my dreams', 'beautiful eyes' and 'hope' point directly too to the heroine.

Another interesting parallel between the two arias comes in the coda of each, strikingly alike in their effect. Rodolfo's ends with a couple of throwaway phrases in which the striking melodic point is a dropping seventh, a rare interval in Puccini melody, where Mimi's ends in exactly comparable throwaway phrases in which the salient interval is a rising seventh. They might be mirror images one of the other, each a quiet appendix rounding off a big aria. The formal balance of the two, contrasted in likeness, is underlined.

That final fragment with its rising seventh appears again in all essentials and very different effect in Mimi's other big aria, her Farewell in Act Three. There, no longer fragmentary, lyrical in the central body of the aria, it accompanies the words *'Involgi tutto quanto'* ('Please put them all together'). Whether or not Puccini intended it as a reference back, it adds to the consistency of the melody given to the heroine. There is comparable consistency in the Fourth Act duet between Rodolfo and Marcello, *'O Mimì, tu più non torni'* ('O Mimi our love is over') [28]. Though it is not actually quoted earlier in the opera, it is

clear enough that the five notes on the words *'tu più non torni'* are closely akin
to the climactic tune in *'Che gelida manina'* [9] and the four descending notes
beginning on *'belli'* directly reflect a salient phrase earlier in that aria on the
words *'e per castelli in aria'*.

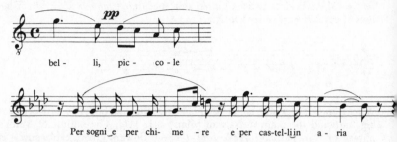

bel - li, pic - co - le

Per sogni_e per chi - me - re   e per cas-tel-li_in   a - ria

Even closer is the parallel with a short section in Act Two, the melody which
comes immediately after the first exposition of Musetta's Waltz Song to the
words *'Ed assaporo allor la bramosia sotil'* ('And with delight I sense their
silent vows of love').

molto rall.

Ed as - sa - po-ro_a-llor la bra - mo - sia sot-til __che da gl'oc chi tra-spi-

How far Puccini was aware of such melodic relationships is hardly material,
let alone whether he intended the listener to register such points. One might as
well ask whether Shakespeare was consciously aware of the consistency of his
imagery within particular plays. What matters is the consistency in the end
result. In *La Bohème* it is a consistency which, the more one studies the score,
increasingly enhances one's admiration for a piece that might on surface
inspection seem superficial.

From the turn of the century and before, every great singer in the Italian
repertory has found inspiration in these characters. If Mimi might seem the
prototype of the Puccinian 'little woman', ostensibly a limited character, the
range of interpretations is astonishing from Melba to Muzio, Victoria de los
Angeles and Maria Callas, whose brittle anguish in Act Three was unforgettable.
More remarkable still is the devotion *La Bohème* has inspired among the
greatest conductors of each generation, plain tribute to the fact that this is not
just a singers' opera but a highly coordinated musical structure. Only *La
Bohème* was recorded complete by both Toscanini and Beecham, the former
electrifying in tension, the latter warmly expansive. Karajan and Solti have
similarly in the present generation paid tribute to the piece in memorable
recordings. If both of them — like Beecham, who claimed to have authority
from the composer himself, but unlike Toscanini, the first ever interpreter —
have tended towards expansiveness, that in itself is a musical tribute. It is one
of the few operas that can never sound pompous however slow the speeds, and
that among other things reflects the strength of the musical argument and its
ease in expressing lightness and humour as well as the heights of passion.

Henry Murger and 'La Vie de Bohème'

Joanna Richardson

The real Bohemian could exist only in Paris. So said Henry Murger, the author of *La Vie de Bohème*; and the observation was true. Nineteenth-century England produced its eccentrics, its aesthetes and its socially unorthodox writers and artists; but there was no sense of a Bohemian movement; there was no Bohemian colony which may be compared with that in Paris. England has never combined the university with the capital, nor fixed so wide a gulf between two classes of men of letters. The English undergraduate in the nineteenth century came, almost certainly, from the upper or middle classes, and he did not know the poverty of the student on the Left Bank. He might be unorthodox in his creeds, extravagant in his behaviour, but he would not lead a tavern life; he would not live on a crust of bread with a sempstress in an attic.

Yet the difference between the English student and his French contemporary was more than a difference of financial status. It was a difference of temperament; and this difference persists at every age. The Frenchman is naturally more inclined than the Englishman to accept the Bohemian way of life, to countenance its idleness, frivolity and passionate intensity. The

Charles Kullman, the American tenor, as Rodolfo at the Met.

Mafalda Favero was an exquisite Mimì at La Scala and the Met. (Teatro alla Scala)

Frenchman, by his nature, is more inclined to indulge in café life, to prolong intellectual conversation. He lacks the matter-of-factness of the Englishman. As Andrew Lang observed, the English character:

> is too domestic, has too little of the gaiety that takes no care for its own morrow, too little of the melancholy that is oppressed by the over-keenly felt sadness of all the forgotten yesterdays and hopeless morrows of all humanity, to produce the sentimental Bohemian.
>
> It is to France, then, that we must turn for studies of this strange kingdom of poetry and lawless art, of loves and duns, of banquets and starvation, informed with a magic that holds youth too often spell-bound with a spell only broken by shameful death.

The moral indignation which Lang expressed in 1908 was no belated Victorian convention. Forty years earlier, in his book *Le Bohème*, Gabriel Guillemot had exposed the false glamour of the Bohemian way of life, and the weaknesses and vices of those who led it. He, too, had insisted that Bohemia was essentially Parisian. As he pointed out:

> The provinces are accustomed to living in broad daylight. They are inquisitive and indiscreet. They have a mania for meddling in their neighbours' affairs. They would not accept a person whose way of life remained problematic or consisted of expedients.
>
> It is only in Paris that you find Bohemia — and even there you don't find it everywhere.
>
> The faubourg Montmartre, the passages, the rue des Martyrs, Notre-Dame-de-Lorette, the whole domain of the unemployed, the debauched and the useless: . . . all this belongs to the realm of Bohemia.
>
> This is almost exclusively its field . . .
>
> You also find it in the place de la Bourse, and in the neighbourhood of the Tuileries and the Champs-Élysées . . .
>
> Occasionally you find it in the Latin Quarter, which used to be its capital . . .

There had been other, sharper attempts to define it on the map: attempts which Murger himself would have accepted. In 1849, the year when *La Vie de Bohème* had first been staged, a writer in *La Silhouette* had pointed out that Bohemia 'was in the department of the Seine. It was bordered on the north by the cold, on the west by hunger, on the south by love, and on the east by hope'. 'Bohemia is a sad country,' wrote Alphonse de Calonne, in *Voyage au Pays de Bohème*. 'It is bordered on the north by need, on the south by misery, on the east by illusion and on the west by the infirmary.'

Bohemian life is in fact a certain way of life in certain quarters of Paris. It begins with the first Bohemia in 1830, the year of literary and political revolution, and one might trace it up to 1914, the year in which, perhaps, the nineteenth century really ended. Even as the nineteenth century drew to its close, the Bohemian principles were growing increasingly difficult to maintain. There was less and less room for the wastrel and the parasite, for those who proclaimed their indifference to the social code. There was less sympathy for the misfit with bogus artistic claims. Bohemianism might remain part of student life, but the adult had to justify Bohemia by proving his artistic genius. Bohemianism could no longer be a permanent escape from maturity.

* * *

Although the nineteenth century was the great age of Bohemia, and few men of letters, few artists and musicians, did not at some time fall beneath its spell,

Antonio Scotti as Marcello. (Royal Opera House Archives)

Edmond Clément as Rodolfo (photo: Nadar)

there is one man who deserves the title of The First Bohemian. He was not the first in time, or the most distinguished, but he gave the word Bohemia its currency. Henry Murger crystallised the impression of Bohemia which has come down to the present day. He fixed a certain vision of the Bohemian way of life, and, rightly or wrongly, he gave it lasting glamour.

Murger was born on March 27, 1822. He was the son of a Parisian concierge (probably of German origin) and an ambitious mother who gave him, if not learning, at least intense respect for what he considered education. Among his father's tenants at 5, rue des Trois-Frères (now 61, rue Taitbout) were Jean-Baptiste Isabey, who had been one of Napoleon's favourite artists; Joseph de Jouy, the Academician and playwright; and Lablache, the tenor, and his daughter. The elderly Monsieur de Jouy used to fill the child with awe and wonder by showing him the toga which Talma, the great actor, had worn in one of his tragedies. Murger was very young when he learned the charm of artistic life.

Ettore Bastianini as Marcello at the Met.
(Royal Opera House Archives)

Tito Gobbi as Marcello (Ida Cook
Collection)

He began to earn his living in prosaic fashion, as a messenger in a solicitor's
office: an occupation which allowed him to idle in the streets, and to compose
his juvenile poetry. Before long, he came to know a group of poverty-stricken
artists and sculptors. Among them were the Desbrosses brothers; their father,
a cab-driver, had turned them out of the house when they chose to follow their
vocations. Joseph, the elder brother, was a sculptor; his spiritual looks and
noble nature led him to be known as 'le Christ'. Leopold, the younger, was an
artist, and he was generally called 'The Gothic'. 'The Desbrosses', wrote
Murger, in the winter of 1814, 'spend half the day not eating and the other half
dying of cold . . . As for a fire, all they have is their pipes — very often without
tobacco.' They had rented a studio at the far end of the rue d'Enfer, and they
later moved to the rue du Cherche-Midi, where their room was heated by the
fumes from the stable below, rising through a hole in the floor.

They were sometimes visited here by Karol: a Bohemian so poor, even by
Bohemian standards, that a thief who waylaid him burst out laughing when he
saw him at closer quarters. Karol's desperate poverty did not prevent him
from being the most generous of friends. It was he who gave Bohemia shelter.
'He did not give it the wherewithal to live, but he gave it the wherewithal not to
die.'

Karol was the son of a soldier of the Grande Armée, who had been wounded at
Wilna, on the retreat from Moscow, and had married the Polish woman who had
looked after him. The family had returned to France, the father had died, and
the mother was left, penniless, to bring up her two sons. Now, in the 1840s, she
ran a little table-d'hôte at thirteen sous in the rue Mignon; and, when all other
expedients failed, like colouring pictures for children, making cheap lithographs,
or carving pipe-stems out of cherry-wood or wild briar, Karol would visit the
rue Mignon for scraps of food.

Karol's love of coffee had reached the proportions of a mania. It was he who gave Murger his passion for coffee, and became — the phrase was Murger's — his Professor of Mocha. Unfortunately Murger, too, carried his coffee-drinking to excess. He nearly always wrote at night, huddled in his attic bed for warmth; and he drank coffee in desperation to keep himself awake. He begged a friend to cure him of this overwhelming addiction. 'I'm literally killing myself. You must cure me. I depend on you.' Some people thought that excessive coffee-drinking was in fact a cause of his premature death.

As a young man, he was already unhealthy; he was also unprepossessing. Philbert Audebrand recalled that his head was Germanic, like his name. His features were clumsy, like those of a mask, and he was prematurely bald. 'His eyes were round, rather like a night bird's; they had a surprised expression, and they were weak.' It was, no doubt to counteract this natural infirmity that Murger wore green spectacles, and, later on, a monocle. His appearance was hardly elegant, at least from 1845 to 1850, and his financial state explained his incorrect dress all too clearly.

This ungainly Bohemian, with the eccentric Karol, and the artists Tabart and Chintreuil, formed a côterie at the hôtel Merciol, in the rue des Canettes. They lived in unbelievable poverty, and exchanged places in hospitals with appalling regularity. If Murger was discharged from Hôpital Saint-Louis, Chintreuil entered it the same day, and he was soon followed by 'The Gothic', who had consumption. 'Le Christ' was exhausted by work and poverty and illness; he spent an entire year in hospital, and died there, of consumption, in 1844. He was twenty-three; some thought that he would have proved himself a quite exceptional artist.

In 1843 the côterie of the hôtel Merciol had formed the society of the *Buveurs-d'eau*, or Water-Drinkers. It was a kind of artistic freemasonry, and its members agreed to advance one another's careers and to help each other in times of particular distress. Each Water-Drinker paid a small subscription into a fund which was used to help the needier members. The fraternity met once a month, and drank water to avoid offending those who were too poor to drink wine.

Murger himself had his moments of unbearable misery. 'We are aching with hunger,' he wrote in 1843, 'we are at the end of our tether. We must find ourselves a niche, or blow our brains out.' Yet Murger was probably the most prosperous of the Water-Drinkers. The solicitor for whom he worked had understandably given him notice, but his old friend M. de Jouy had found him a post as secretary to a certain Count Tolstoy. The Count, a Russian émigré, had been implicated in a plot against the Czar some twenty years earlier; he was now trying to redeem himself by acting as an unofficial diplomat in Paris. He paid Murger forty francs a month.

However, Murger was more than thankful to discover a café where a cup of coffee cost 5 sous; it was the Café Momus, in the rue des Prêtres-Saint-Germain-l'Auxerrois, and he began to spend his evenings there. He was joined by his friend Alexandre Schanne. Schanne was a year his junior, his parents were toy-manufacturers, and he himself had learned painting from the historical painter Léon Cogniet. Now he scraped a living together by selling pictures to junk-shops, giving piano lessons, and playing the violin at the Théâtre-Lyrique. He even played the trombone at the Élysée-Montmartre.

Once Murger and Schanne became regular patrons of the Café Momus, the quiet smoking-room became unbearable for bourgeois customers. In his book *Scènes de la Bohème* Murger was to embroider on the subject:

In those days, Gustave Colline, the great philosopher, Marcel, the great painter, Schaunard, the great musician, and Rodolphe, the great poet, as they used to call one another, reguarly frequented the Café Momus.

Geraldine Farrar as Mimì at the Met.   *Frances Alda as Mimì at the Met. in 1917.*

They were known as The Four Musketeers, because they were always seen together; and in fact they came and went together, gambled together, and sometimes failed to pay their bills, also with an *ensemble* which was worthy of the Conservatoire.

They had chosen to meet in a room which would comfortably have held forty people; but they were always by themselves, because they had finally made the place unapproachable to ordinary customers.

The passing client who ventured into the den . . . used to escape without finishing his paper or his coffee (the unheard-of aphorisms on art, feeling and political economy turned the cream sour). Such were the conversations of the four friends that the waiter who served them had gone mad . . .

There were in fact more than four Bohemians at the Café Momus; thanks to the cheap coffee and the stimulating company, an army of writers and artists soon turned the smoking-room into a sort of Bohemian club. Among them, wearing his inevitable jonquil-coloured coat and brown cravat, was Murger's friend Champfleury, who would, one day, disown his Bohemian ways. When a critic ventured to call him King of Bohemia, Champfleury retorted that he was neither the king nor a subject. 'No-one who lives by his pen, however modestly, is,' he said, 'a Bohemian.' For him the Bohemian was an ignorant wastrel, an idler of dubious morality. He himself earned a reputation as a novelist and art historian, and finally became Director of the State porcelain factory at Sèvres.

In the days of the Café Momus, however, Champfleury was undoubtedly Bohemian. He consorted with the versatile and ubiquitous Nadar; and with them were Gustave Courbet, the young painter from Ornans; Baudelaire, and the grim and desperate writer Charles Barbara, whom he befriended. There were Charles Monselet, a journalist fresh from the provinces, and Antoine Fauchery. Some of the less scrupulous Bohemians found a scheme whereby the first arrival ordered a cup of coffee; and all the others joined him, read the papers, played backgammon, and monopolised the smoking-room for the initial outlay of five sous. By great good fortune the proprietor of the Café Momus had literary dreams of his own; he sympathised with the uproarious and at times dishonest clientèle, and could not bring himself to turn them out.

* * *

Catherine Mastio as Mimi

Emma Trentini as Musetta at the
Manhattan Opera House in 1906

On February 18, 1845, in a letter to a friend, Murger himself announced his first steps to fame. 'I have tossed a dozen anecdotes or so into the letter-box of *Le Corsaire*, and I shall now enjoy seeing them in print.' The first anecdote of Bohemian life was published in *Le Corsaire* on March 9. This, and the ones which followed, were to be the basis of Murger's book, *Scènes de la Bohème*.

The second article was printed almost a year after the first: on March 6, 1846. It described how Rodolphe, a poet, won the love of a little grisette called Louise. The article was thinly disguised autobiography. Rodolphe was clearly Murger himself, and Louise was almost certainly inspired by Lucile Louvet, a factory-girl whom he had come to know. Lucile (who made artificial flowers) was undoubtedly the model for Mimi, who first appeared in the third of Murger's sketches on July 9, 1846. Thenceforward, Murger gave his readers regular accounts of his own liaison; and, in 1847, he made copy of the end of the affair. His behaviour was calculating, and it was distasteful; but he remained desperate for money. In 1848 he was forced to ask the editor of *Le Corsaire* for five francs to buy food. In June that year, writing from hospital, he begged him to advance him a few sous, and swore by Ricord, the famous surgeon, that he would send him copy twice a week. It was in these conditions — not in any Romantic Bohemia — that he drove himself to write his masterpiece. The last instalment of *Scènes de la Bohème* appeared some four years after the first: in April 1849.

It was not the first time that the word Bohemia had been used to describe an irregular way of life. Balzac had used it in 1830 to describe the setting of his novel *Un Grand Homme de Province à Paris*, and Gautier had already used the term to describe the inhabitants of the Impasse de Doyenné. But such points remain academic. Murger was the first writer to live the true Bohemian life and to give a faithful description of it.

His characters certainly owed much to his friends and acquaintances. While he himself was said to be Rodolphe, and Lucile Louvet and several other women he had known had gone to the making of Mimi, Musette (like the heroine of Champfleury's later novel, *Les Aventures de Mademoiselle Mariette*), was based on one of the wild Queens of Bohemia, Marie-Christine Roux. 'Her wit was genuine,' went her obituary, 'and her voice was remarkably melodious. She expressed herself with a purity which gave no hint

39

of her lack of education.' It is not known if she recognised herself in *Scènes de la Bohème*; but it is said that she was 'not exactly grateful to M. Champfleury for the novel which gave her celebrity'. She was drowned when the *Atlas* went down between Marseilles and Oran in December 1863.

Alexandre Schanne, in his memoirs, identified Murger's Barbemuche as Charles Barbara, and Colline as a combination of Jean Wallon and Marc Trapadoux. Wallon was an inveterate book-hunter, and a tireless student of philosophy; in time he became an official, and towards the end of the Second Empire he became Directeur de l'Imprimerie impériale. But till the end of his life he was proud of his part as the bibliophile in *Scènes de la Bohème*. As for the other Bohemian who inspired the character of Colline, he was a tall, bearded man with a vague resemblance to Michelangelo. He appeared several times in Courbet's paintings: once in the crowd in the artist's studio, at other times alone, reading a book or leafing through a portfolio of engravings. His name — quite as strange as the man himself — was Marc Trapadoux. If he had a profession, no-one knew it. But he came every day to the Café Momus.

* * *

Scènes de la Bohème had begun to appear in *Le Corsaire* in 1845. Murger was paid fifteen francs an article. But though the *feuilletons* were appreciated by his fellow-writers, Murger's popular success was only to come when the work was adapted for the stage. Théodore Barrière was a young clerk at the Ministry of War. He had already had a number of vaudevilles performed, but he still needed to make his name. He recognised the dramatic possibilities of *Scènes de la Bohème*, and he asked Fauchery to introduce him to the author.

La Vie de Bohème, by Henry Murger and Théodore Barrière, was first performed at the Théâtre des Variétés on November 22, 1849. It was greeeted with enthusiasm; its novelty, its picturesqueness, its free-and-easy way of life were presented with wit and gusto and gaiety. 'As long as men and women are young, and not quite virtuous,' Arthur Symons, the English poet, wrote, years later, 'so long will this kind of life exist . . . ; and never has it been rendered so sympathetically, and with so youthful a touch of sentiment . . . To be five-and-twenty, poor and in love: that is enough; at that age, and in those circumstances, you will feel that Murger has said everything.'

On the evening of the première of *La Vie de Bohème*, the publisher Michel Lévy took both its authors to supper at the Maison d'Or. He offered Murger five hundred francs in gold, on the spot, if he would gather his stories from *Le Corsaire* into a book, and give him all the rights. Murger accepted. Within a few days, he had moved to an apartment on the Right Bank. 'Would you believe it?' said Théodore de Banville. 'Nowadays that lucky Murger peels his pippins with silver-handled knives!'

While many bourgeois had secretly aspired to be Bohemian, Murger himself had longed to be a bourgeois; and his change of address was symbolic. His move to the Right Bank was recognised as a public rejection of Bohemia; and the following year, in the preface to his book for Michel Lévy, he confirmed, emphatically, that his own Bohemian days were over. 'Bohemia,' he wrote, 'is a stage in artistic life; it is the preface to the Académie, to the Hôtel-Dieu or the Morgue.' If Bohemia sometimes led to Academic glory, it led all too frequently to the poor-house, or to death. Murger himself had no illusions. He became increasingly conventional, and he was duly awarded the seal of respectability: the cross of Chevalier de la Légion-d'honneur. But he had always been unhealthy, and years of desperate poverty had taken their toll. On January 28, 1861, he died at the Maison Dubois. He was thirty-eight. His last words were: 'No music, no noise, . . . no Bohemia, *no Bohemia!*'

Thematic Guide

Many of the themes from the opera have been identified in the articles by numbers in square brackets, which refer to the themes set out on these pages. The themes are also identified by the numbers in brackets at the corresponding points in the libretto, so that the words can be related to the musical themes.

[1] *The Bohemians*
Allegro vivace

[2] **RODOLFO**
Allegro vivace

Look how the smoke is laz - i - ly float - ing
Nei cie - li bi - gi guar - do fu - mar dai

up from the stoves all o - ver Par - is!
mil - le co - mi - gno - li Pa - ri - gi, —

[3] *Colline*
Allegro vivace

[4] *Schaunard*
Allegro

[10] **MIMI**

Andante lento

I'm al - ways called Mi - mi
Mi chia - ma - no Mi - mi

[11] **MIMI**

Andante calmo

These flow - ers give me pleas - ure   as in mag - i - cal ac - cents
Mi piac - cion quel - le co - se   che han si dol - ce ma - li - a,

rit.

They speak to me   of love, of   love - ly spring - time. _____
che par - la - no   d'a - mor, di   pri - ma - ve - ra. _____

[12a] **MIMI**

Allegretto moderato *con semplicità*

All   by my - self   I   have my fru - gal sup - per;
So - la,   mi fo   il   pran - zo da me stes - sa.

I   go   to Mass but   sel - dom
Non   va - do sem - pre a   mes - sa

[12b]

Andantino

43

[13]

[14] *The Hawkers*

Come buy my o - ran - ges! Hot roast - ed chest - nuts.
A - ran - ci, dat - te - ri! Cal - di i ma - ro - ni.

[15] *Musetta*

[16] *Musetta*

[17] MUSETTA

As through the street __ as through the street I wan - der on my way
Quan - do me'n vo', __ quan -do me'n vo so - let - ta per la via

the peo - ple turn to look at me.
la gen - te so - sta e mi - ra.

[18] *Tattoo*

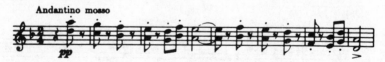

[19]

Andantino mosso

44

[20] TAVERN CHORUS

Andantino mosso

dolce e con grazia

Fill the glass! Each toast his love.
Chi nel ber tro - vo il pia - cer,

[21]

Andante

[22] RODOLFO

Allegro moderato *with bitter irony*

Mi - mi is fic - kle heart - ed, al - ways flirt - ing with some - one.
Mi - mi è u - na ci - vet - ta ___ che fra - scheg - gia con tut - ti.

[23] RODOLFO

Lento triste

Mi - mi's so sick - ly, so ail - ing, Ev' - ry day she grows weak - er.
Mi - mi è tan - to ma - la - ta! O - gni dì più de - cli - na.

[24] RODOLFO

Sostenuto molto

By fierce in - ces - sant cough - ing her frail be - ing is
U - na ter - ri - bil tos - se l'e - sil pet - to le

sha - ken ___
scuo - te ___

[25]

Andante con moto

45

[26] **MIMI**

Andante con moto

Fare - well, a - wak - ing be - side you when day is break - ing
Ad - di - o dol - ce sve - glia - re al - la mat - ti - na

[27] **MIMI AND RODOLFO**

Andante con moto   *poco allargando*

Lone - ly in win - ter with death as sole com - pan - ion!
So - li l'in - ver - no è co - sa da mo - ri - re

[28] **RODOLFO**

Andantino mosso

O Mi - mi our love is o - ver.
O Mi - mi tu più non tor - ni.

Oh days de - part - ed,
O gior - ni bel - li,

[29] **SCHAUNARD** / *The Quadrille Grazioso*

Lal - le - ra, lal - le - ra, lal - le - ra, là, lal - le - ra, lal - le - ra, lal - le - ra, là.

[30] **COLLINE**

Moderato e triste

Ven - er - able gar - ment, lis - ten I'll say good - bye
Vec - chia zi - mar - ra sen - ti, io re - sto al pian

[31] **MIMI**

Andante calmo

Have they left us? I was not real - ly sleep - ing
So - no an - da - ti? Fin - ge - vo di dor - mi - re

but I want - ed to be a - lone with you, love
per - chè vol - li con te so - la re - sta - re

46

La Bohème

Opera in Four Acts by Giacomo Puccini
Libretto by Giuseppe Giacosa and Luigi Illica
after Henry Murger's
'Scènes de la Vie de Bohème'

English version of Acts One and Two
by William Grist and Percy Pinkerton
Acts Three and Four by Percy Pinkerton

La Bohème was first performed at the Teatro Regio, Turin, on February 1, 1896. It was first performed in England by the Carl Rosa Opera Company at the Theatre Royal, Manchester, on April 22, 1897 in the original Grist/ Pinkerton translation. The first performance in London was also in English, at Covent Garden on October 2, 1897. The first Italian performance at Covent Garden was on July 1, 1899. It was first performed in the USA in Los Angeles on October 14, 1897, and then in New York on May 16, 1898.

This English text is the result of many years of performance alterations. The first lines of the famous arias have remained untouched but almost every other line has been altered.

The stage directions (and opening quotations from Murger) are part of this translation and do not reflect any particular production.

Ricordi published the text by Giacosa and Illica at the time of the first performances. This forms the basis for the verse layout of this libretto in both languages. The words which Puccini actually set to music vary considerably from that text, however, and, because all his alterations have been incorporated here, the verse has been lost in many places in a welter of exclamations and simultaneous dialogue.

THE CHARACTERS

Marcello *a painter*	*baritone*
Rodolfo *a poet*	*tenor*
Colline *a philosopher*	*bass*
Schaunard *a musician*	*baritone*
Benoit *a landlord*	*bass*
Mimi *a seamstress*	*soprano*
Parpignol *an itinerant toy-seller*	*tenor*
Musetta *a singer*	*soprano*
Alcindoro *a state councillor and admirer of Musetta*	*bass*
Customs Sergeant	*bass*
Customs Official	

Street Vendors, Students, Citizens, Children and Peasants

Paris, about 1830.

. . . rain or dust, cold or heat, nothing stops these bold adventurers . . .

Their existence of every day is a work of genius, a daily problem which they always contrive to solve with the aid of bold mathematics . . .

When want presses them, abstemious as anchorites — but if a little fortune falls into their hands see them ride forth on the most ruinous fancies, loving the fairest and youngest, drinking the oldest and best wines and not finding enough windows whence to throw their money; then — the last sovereign dead and buried — they begin again to dine at the 'table d'hôte' of chance where their cover is always laid; contrabandists of all the industries which spring from art, hunting from morning till night that wild animal which is called the sovereign.

'Bohemia' has a special dialect, a distinct jargon of its own. . . This vocabulary is the hell of rhetoric and the paradise of neologism.

. . . .
. . . .

A gay life, yet a terrible one! . . .

H. MURGER, preface to the 'Vie de Bohème'

Rather than follow Murger's novel step by step, the authors of the present libretto, for reasons of both musical and dramatic effect, have sought to derive inspiration from the French writer's admirable preface.

Although they have faithfully portrayed the characters, even displaying a certain fastidiousness as to sundry local details; albeit in the scenic development of the opera they have followed Murger's method by dividing the libretto into four separate acts, in the dramatic and comic episodes they have claimed that ample and entire freedom of action which (rightly or wrongly) they deemed necessary to the proper stage presentation of a novel which is, perhaps, the most free in modern literature.

Yet in this strange book, if the characters of each person therein stand out clear and sharply defined, we may often perceive that one and the same temperament bears different names, and that it is incarnated, so to speak, in two different persons. Who cannot detect in the delicate profile of one woman the personality both of Mimì and of Françine? Who as he reads of Mimì's "little hands, whiter than those of the Goddess of Ease", is not reminded of Françine's little muff?

The authors deem it their duty to point out this identity of character. It has seemed to them that those two mirthful, fragile and unhappy creatures in this comedy of Bohemian life might aptly figure as one person whose name should be, not Mimì, not Françine, but "The Ideal".

G.G. — L.I.

. . . Mimi was a charming girl specially apt to appeal to Rodolfo, the poet and dreamer. Aged twenty-two, she was slight and graceful. Her face reminded one of some sketch of a highborn beauty; its features had marvellous refinement . . .

The hot and impetuous blood of youth coursed through her veins, giving a rosy hue to her clear complexion that had the white velvety bloom of the camellia . . .

This frail beauty allured Rodolfo . . . But what wholly served to enchant him were Mimi's tiny hands, that, despite her household duties, she contrived to keep whiter even than those of the Goddess of Ease.

A scene from the first performance in Turin in 1896.

Act One

In the Attic.

A spacious window from which one sees an expanse of snow-clad roofs, on the left a stove. A table, a small cupboard, a little book-case, four chairs, a picture easel, a bed; a few books, many packs of cards, two candlesticks. A door in the middle; another on the left. [1]

Rodolfo — Marcello

(Rodolfo looks pensively out of the window. Marcello works at his painting 'The Passage of the Red Sea' with hands nipped with cold, and warms them by blowing on them from time to time, often changing position, on account of the frost.)

MARCELLO
(seated, continuing to paint)

This Red Sea Passage feels damp and chill to me.	Questo Mar Rosso — mi ammollisce e assidera
As if a stream down my back were flowing.	come se addosso — mi piovesse in stille.

(He goes a little way back from the easel to look at the picture.)

But, in revenge a Pharaoh will I drown!	Per vendicarmi, affogo un Faraon!

(He turns to his work.)

And you?	Che fai?

RODOLFO

Look how the smoke is [2]	Nei cieli bigi
lazily floating up from	guardo fumar dai mille
the stoves all over Paris.	comignoli Parigi,

(pointing to the fireless stove)

And yet that stove beside us	e penso a quel poltrone
does nothing more to earn an honest living	d'un vecchio caminetto ingannatore
than lie in idleness just like a lord!	che vive in ozio come un gran signor!

MARCELLO

It's a very long time since	Le sue rendite oneste
we paid his lawful wages.	da un pezzo non riceve.

RODOLFO

Of what use are those forests,	Quelle sciocche foreste
all white under the snow?	che fan sotto la neve?

MARCELLO

Rodolfo, let me tell you a thought that overwhelms me:	Rodolfo, io voglio dirti un mio pensier profondo:
I'm simply frozen.	ho un freddo cane.

RODOLFO
(approaching Marcello)

And I, Marcel, to be quite candid	Ed io, Marcel, non ti nascondo
have no faith in the sweat on my forehead.	che non credo al sudor della fronte.

MARCELLO

All my fingers	Ho ghiacciate
are frozen. Just as if they'd been touching that iceberg,	le dita quasi ancor le tenessi immollate
touching that block of marble, the heart of false Musetta!	giù in quella gran ghiacciaia che è il cuore di Musetta!

(He heaves a long sigh, laying aside his palette and brushes, and ceases painting.)

RODOLFO

Ah! Love's a stove that squanders a lot of fuel . . .	L'amor è un caminetto che sciupa troppo . . .

MARCELLO

... too quickly!   ... e in fretta!

RODOLFO

Where the man does the burning ...   ... dove l'uomo è fascina ...

MARCELLO

... and the woman the lighting.   ... e la donna è l'alare ...

RODOLFO

As the one becomes ashes ...   ... l'uno brucia in un soffio ...

MARCELLO

... the other stands and watches.   ... e l'altro sta a guardare.

RODOLFO

But meanwhile here we're freezing ...   Ma intanto qui si gela ...

MARCELLO

... and we're dying of hunger!   ... e si muore d'inedia!

RODOLFO

We must have fire ...   Fuoco ci vuole ...

MARCELLO
(seizing a chair and about to break it up)

I have it! This will be our salvation.   Aspetta ... sacrifichiam la sedia!
(Rodolfo energetically resists Marcello's project.)

RODOLFO
(delighted with an idea which has seized him)

Eureka!   Eureka!
(He runs to the table and picks up a bulky manuscript.)

MARCELLO

You've found it?   Trovasti?

RODOLFO

Yes! When genius   Si. Aguzza
is wakened, ideas come fast and furious.   l'ingegno. L'idea vampi in fiamma.

MARCELLO
(pointing to his picture)

Let's burn the Red Sea!   Bruciamo il Mar Rosso?

RODOLFO

No. Think of   No. Puzza
the smell it would make here. But my   la tela dipinta. Il mio dramma,
drama,
my beautiful drama shall give us warmth.   l'ardente mio dramma ci scaldi.

MARCELLO
(with comic terror)

You're not going to read it. You'll freeze   Vuoi leggerlo forse? Mi geli.
me.

RODOLFO

No, the paper in flame shall be burning;   No, in cener la carta si sfaldi
the soul to its heaven returning.   e l'estro rivoli ai suoi cieli.
(with importance)
Great loss, but the world yet must bear it   Al secol gran danno minaccia ...
for Rome is in peril!   è Roma in periglio!

MARCELLO

Great soul!   Gran cor!

RODOLFO

(He gives Marcello a portion of the manuscript.)

Let's start with the first act. A te l'atto primo.

MARCELLO

Right! Qua.

RODOLFO

Tear it. Straccia.

MARCELLO

And light it. Accendi.

(Rodolfo strikes a flint on steel, lights a candle and goes to the stove with Marcello; together they set fire to a part of the manuscript thrown into the fire-basket then both draw up their chairs and sit down, happily warming themselves.)

RODOLFO

How cheerful the blaze! Che lieto baglior!

MARCELLO

How cheerful the blaze! Che lieto baglior!

(The door at the back opens violently and Colline enters frozen stiff, stamping his feet and angrily throwing on the table a bundle of books.) [3]

Rodolfo — Marcello — Colline

COLLINE

Surely the day of judgement would seem to be dawning! Già dell'Apocalisse appariscono i segni.

On Christmas Eve they will not take my volumes for pawning! In giorno di Vigilia non si accettano pegni!

(He checks himself, seeing the fire in the stove.)

What are you burning? Una fiammata!

RODOLFO
(to Colline)

Gently, for that's my drama . . . Zitto, si da il mio dramma . . .

MARCELLO

. . . in action. . . . al fuoco.

COLLINE

Indeed I find it sparkling. Lo trovo scintillante.

RODOLFO

Brilliant. Vivo.

(The fire languishes)

MARCELLO

Too short its phrases. Ma dura poco.

RODOLFO

Brevity's deemed a virtue. La brevità, gran pregio.

COLLINE
(taking the chair from Rodolfo)

Your chair if you'll permit me. Autore, a me la sedia.

MARCELLO

These endless pauses make us die of boredom. Quickly! Quest' intermezzi fan morir dinedia. Presto.

RODOLFO
(taking another portion of the manuscript)

Here is the next act. Atto secondo.

MARCELLO
(*to Colline*)

Hush, not a whisper.   Non far sussurro.

(*Rodolfo tears up the manuscript and throws part of it into the stove; the flame revives. Colline moves his chair nearer and warms his hands. Rodolfo is standing near them with the rest of the manuscript.*)

COLLINE
(*as if a theatre critic*)

Profound and thoughtful.   Pensier profondo!

MARCELLO

Solemn and wise.   Giusto color!

RODOLFO

In that blue smoke my drama is dying   In quell'azzurro — giuzzo languente
full of the ardent yearning of love.   sfuma un'ardente — scena d'amor.

COLLINE

What fiery pages.   Scoppietta un foglio.

MARCELLO

There! Those were kisses!   Là c'eran baci!

RODOLFO

Three acts at once I desire to hear.   Tre atti or voglio — d'un colpo udir.

(*He throws the remaining manuscript on the fire.*)

COLLINE

Only the daring can dream such visions. Tal degli audaci — l'idea s'integra.

ALL

Dreams that in bright flame soon disappear. Bello in allegra — vampa svanir.

(*They applaud enthusiastically; the fire dies.*)

MARCELLO

Ye Gods! See the leaves nearly perished! Oh! Dio ... già s'abbassa la fiamma.

COLLINE

How vain is the drama we cherished!   Che vano, che fragile dramma!

MARCELLO

They crackle, they curl up and die!   Già scricchiola, increspasi, muor!

COLLINE AND MARCELLO

The Author! Now, down with him we cry! Abbasso, sì, abbasso l'autor!

(*From the middle door enter two boys, one carrying food, wine and cigars, the other a bundle of wood. At the noise, the three at the fire turn round, and with a cry of wonder they fall upon the provisions brought by the boys and deposit them on the table; Colline takes the wood and carries it near the stove.*) [4]

COLLINE

Firewood!   Legna!

MARCELLO

Cigars!   Sigari!

RODOLFO

Bordeaux!   Bordò!

ALL THREE

All the luxury of Christmas   Le dovizie d'una fiera
we are fated yet to know.   il destin ci destinò.

(*Exeunt the two boys.*)

SCHAUNARD
(He enters with a triumphant air, throwing some coins on the ground.)

These riches I bring you will break the Bank of France.	La Banca di Francia per voi si sbilancia.

COLLINE
(picking up the coins together with Rodolfo and Marcello)

Collect them! Collect them!	Raccatta, racatta!

MARCELLO
(incredulous)

Just pieces of metal!	Son pezzi di latta!...

SCHAUNARD
(showing him a coin)

You're stupid ... or blind? What face do they show?	Sei sordo?... Sei lippo? Quest'uomo chi è?

RODOLFO
(bowing)

King Louis Philippe! To my monarch I bow.	Luigi Filippo! M'inchino al mio Re!

ALL

Shall King Louis Philippe at our feet lie low?	Sta Luigi Filippo ai nostri piè!

(Schaunard continues to recount his good luck; but the others do not listen to him and go on arranging everything and putting wood in the stove.)

SCHAUNARD

Now I'll explain; this gold here, or rather silver has its own noble story.	Or vi dirò: quest'oro, o meglio, argento ha la sua brava storia ...

RODOLFO

Let us heat up the furnace.	Riscaldiamo il camino!

COLLINE

So much cold has it suffered.	Tanto freddo ho sofferto!

SCHAUNARD

'Twas an English milord, Lord ... or a duke or something, required a musician.	Un inglese ... un signor ... Lord o Milord che sia, volea un musicista ...

MARCELLO
(throwing Colline's books off the table)

Off! Let us set up the table!	Via! Prepariamo la tavola!

SCHAUNARD

I fly there!	Io? volo.

RODOLFO

Where is the food?	L'esca dov'è?

COLLINE

There!	Là.

MARCELLO

Here!	Qua.

SCHAUNARD

I bow before him. He nods and then I asked him.	E mi presento. M'accetta; gli domando ...

COLLINE
(arranging the viands)

Here's some roast beef.	Arrosto freddo!

MARCELLO

Delicious pastry!	Pasticcio dolce!

SCHAUNARD

When shall we start the lessons?	A quando le lezioni? . . .

MARCELLO
(He lights the candles and puts them on the table.)

Here are the candles.	Or le candele!

SCHAUNARD

He answers right away.	Risponde: 'Incominciam! . . . '
'Just look there': pointing upstairs to a parrot in his cage,	*'Guardare!'* (e un pappagallo m'addita al primo pian)
he commands me, 'You must play until	poi soggiunge: *'Voi suonare*
that bird dies of terror'. And so it was:	*finché quello morire!'* E fu così:
three days I played and yelled.	Suonai tre lunghi dì . . .
Then on the servant girl try all	Allora usai l'incanto
my charm and fascination . . .	di mia presenza bella . . .
I captivate the maiden . . .	Affascinai l'ancella . . .
I tempt the bird with parsley . . .	Gli propinai prezzemolo! . . .
and then his wings out-spreading,	Lorito allargò l'ali,
the parrot opened his beak,	lorito il becco aprì,
A little piece of parsley,	un poco di prezzemolo,
and as Socrates he died.	da Socrate morì!

RODOLFO

Brilliantly lightens the room into splendour.	Fulgida folgori la sala spendida.

MARCELLO

Here are the candles.	Or le candele.

COLLINE

Wonderful pudding!	Pasticcio dolce!

MARCELLO

No cloth here on the table?	Mangiar senza tovaglia?

RODOLFO

An idea.	Un'idea! . . .

(He takes a newspaper from his pocket.)

COLLINE AND MARCELLO

The Paris evening news.	*Il Costituzional!*

RODOLFO
(explaining)

Excellent paper!	Ottima carta . . .
One eats a meal and swallows news together.	Si mangia e si divora un'appendice!

(Seeing that no one is listening, Schaunard grasps Colline as he passes with a plate.)

COLLINE

Who?	Chi?! . . .

SCHAUNARD
(pettishly)

The devil take the lot of you to Hades.	Il diavolo vi porti tutti quanti!

(seeing the rest about to eat the cold pie)

What are you doing?	Ed or che fate?

(With a solemn gesture he extends his hand over the pie.)

No! Dainties of this kind	No! Queste cibarie
are to be saved for later,	sono la salmeria
saved for the morrow	pei dì futuri

fraught with gloom and sorrow.	tenebrosi e oscuri.

(clearing the table as he speaks)

To dine at home	Pranzare in casa
on this eve of Christmas?	il dì della Vigilia
While in the Latin Quarter bright cafés	mentre il Quartier Latino le sue vie
display their sweetmeats, rich and full of relish.	addobba di salsicce e leccornie?
Meanwhile the smell of savoury dishes perfumes the town	[13] Quando un'olezzo di frittelle imbalsama
with fragrant odour.	le vecchie strade?
There, singing joyously, pretty maidens hover.	Là le ragazze cantano contente –

THE OTHERS

On this merry Christmas Eve!	La vigilia di Natal!

SCHAUNARD

Each girl is seeking for a student lover!	ed han per eco ognuna uno studente!
You must be more religious my friends I beg you.	Un po' di religione, o miei signori:
We drink at home but go out to dine.	si beva in casa, ma si pranzi fuor.

(Rodolfo locks the door; then they all go to the table and pour out the wine; someone knocks at the door; they are surprised.)

Rodolfo — Marcello — Colline — Schaunard — later Benoit

BENOIT
(off-stage)

It's me!	Si può?

MARCELLO

Who is that?	Chi è là?

BENOIT

Benoit.	Benoit.

MARCELLO

That's the voice of the landlord!	Il padrone di casa!

SCHAUNARD

Bolt the door quickly!	Uscio sul muso.

COLLINE
(calling)

No-one at home.	Non c'è nessuno.

SCHAUNARD

I've locked it.	É chiuso.

BENOIT

Give me a word, pray.	Una parola.

SCHAUNARD
(After consulting his friends, he opens the door.)

Only one!	Sola!

BENOIT
(He enters smiling; he sees Marcello and shows him a paper.)

Rent!	Affitto!

MARCELLO
(with exaggerated cordiality)

Hallo!	Olà!
Give him a seat, friends.	Date una sedia.

RODOLFO

Quickly.	Presto.

BENOIT
(defending himself)

Do not trouble, I beg you.   Non occurre. Vorrei . . .

SCHAUNARD
(With gentle firmness he insists that Benoit sits.)

There now.   Segga.

MARCELLO

Some wine, sir.   Vuol bere?
(He pours him some wine.)

BENOIT

Thank you.   Grazie.

RODOLFO AND COLLINE

Your health.   Tocchiamo.

(All drink. Benoit puts down his glass and turns to Marcello showing him the paper.)

BENOIT

It's   Questo
the quarter's rent I call for,   è l'ultimo trimestre . . .

MARCELLO
(ingenuously)

Glad to hear it.   Ne ho piacere.

BENOIT

And therefore . . .   E quindi . . .

SCHAUNARD
(interrupting him)

Another glass, sir.   Ancora un sorso.
(He refills the glasses)

BENOIT

Thank you.   Grazie.

ALL FOUR
(touching Benoit's glass)

Here's to your good health, sir!   Alla sua salute!

BENOIT
(addressing Marcello)

To you I come as   A lei ne vengo
the quarter now is ended.   perchè il trimestre scorso
You had promised . . .   mi promise . . .

MARCELLO

And I shall keep my promise.   Promisi ed or mantengo.
(showing Benoit the coins on the table)

RODOLFO
(aside to Marcello)

What's this?   Che fai? . . .

SCHAUNARD
(aside to the others)

You idiot!   Sei pazzo?

MARCELLO
(to Benoit, ignoring the other two)

You've seen it. Then lay   Ha visto? Or via
all care aside, sir, and join our friendly circle.   resti un momento in nostra compagnia.
Tell me how old you are,   Dica: quant'anni ha,
my dear monsieur Benoit?   caro signor Benoit?

BENOIT

My age! Spare me, I pray!   Gli anni? . . . Per carità!

RODOLFO

Our own age, less or more?   Su e giù la nostra età.

BENOIT
(*protesting*)

Much more, very much more.   Di più, molto di più.

(*While they make Benoit chatter they fill up his glass as soon as it is empty.*)

COLLINE

You're very frank, I'm sure.   Ha detto su e giù.

MARCELLO
(*lowering his voice and in a mischievous tone*)

The other evening at Mabille . . . I caught   L'altra sera al Mabil . . . L'hanno colto
him
with a girl in his arms.   in peccato d'amor!

BENOIT
(*uneasy*)

Me?   Io?

MARCELLO

Deny it.   Neghi.

BENOIT

The chance came.   Un caso.

MARCELLO
(*flattering him*)

She was lovely.   Bella donna!

BENOIT
(*half-drunk, suddenly*)

Delightful.   Ah! molto.

SCHAUNARD
(*He slaps him on the shoulder.*)

Old rascal!   Briccone!

COLLINE

Vile seducer!   Seduttore!

(*He slaps him on the other shoulder.*)

MARCELLO
(*exaggerating*)

Casanova! Don Giovanni!   Una quercia! . . . un cannone!

BENOIT

Ha! Ha!   Ha! Ha!

RODOLFO

He's quite discerning.   L'uomo ha buon gusto.

MARCELLO

Her hair was curly auburn.   Il crin ricciuto, fulvo.
Aflame with passion he seizes her and   [5] Ei gongolava arzillo, pettoruto.
tames her.

BENOIT
(*getting more and more carried away*)

I'm ancient, but I'm sturdy.   Son vecchio, ma robusto.

59

Flaming with love he teases her and shames her.

Ei gongolava arzuto e pettorillo.

MARCELLO

To him she yields her maiden's innocence.

E'a lui cedea, le femminil virtù.

BENOIT
(very confidentially)

I was a timid youth	Timido in gioventù,
but now I'm getting even. You know that my one delight	ora me ne ripago ... Si sa, è uno svago
is a merry lady ... You know ...	qualche donnetta allegra ... e un po' ...
I do not want a whale,	Non dico una balena,
or a globe to study.	o un mappamondo,
Nor like a full moon,	o un viso tondo
a face round and ruddy,	da luna piena,
but leanness, downright leanness, no, no, no!	ma magra, proprio magra, no e poi no!
It is a lean woman's satisfaction	Le donne magre sono grattacapi
to drive us to distraction.	e spesso sopracapi ...
Full of wrangling and strife,	e son piene di doglie,
as for instance my wife ...	per esempio mia moglie ...

(Marcello bangs his fist down on the table; the others follow his example; Benoit looks at them in bewilderment.)

MARCELLO
(very angrily)

This man is married	Quest'uomo ha moglie
yet harbours lustful	e sconcie voglie
desires!	ha nel cor!

SCHAUNARD, COLLINE

For shame!

Orror!

RODOLFO

His vile pollution	E ammorba, e appesta
empoisons our honest	la nostra onesta
abode.	magion.

SCHAUNARD, COLLINE

Out!

Fuor!

MARCELLO

With perfume we must fumigate!

Si abbruci dello succhero!

COLLINE

Drive him out, the reprobate!

Si discacci il reprobo!

SCHAUNARD
(imperiously)

Morality offended drives you from us!

É la morale offesa che vi scaccia!

BENOIT
(vainly trying to speak)

I say ... I say ...

Io di ... io di ...

COLLINE, RODOLFO

Be silent!

Silenzio!

BENOIT
(more and more bewildered)

Sirs, I beg you!

Miei signori ...

60

MARCELLO, SCHAUNARD, COLLINE
(surrounding Benoit, and pushing him towards the door)

Be silent! Out your lordship,   Silenzio! via Signore, via di qua!
   (They push Benoit out of the door, and then they stand looking down the staircase:)
We wish your Lordship a pleasant Christ-   E buona sera a vostra signoria.
mas Eve.

(laughing)

Ha! Ha! Ha! Ha!   Ah! Ah! Ah! Ah!

MARCELLO
(closing the door)

    That has settled the rent!   Ho pagato il trimestre!

SCHAUNARD

And now off to Momus where dinner   Al Quartiere Latin ci attende Momus.
awaits.

MARCELLO

Long live the spendthrift!   Viva chi spende!

SCHAUNARD

    Let us all take our share!   Dividiamo il bottin!

(They divide the money on the table.)

MARCELLO
(holding out a cracked mirror to Colline)

Girls await you there, angels from heaven.   Là ci son beltà scese dal cielo.
Now you are rich, to decency pay tribute.   Or che sei ricco, bada alla decenza!
Bear! Go and get your hair cut.   Orso, ravviati il pelo.

COLLINE

I'll scrape my first acquaintance   Farò la conoscenza
this very day with some tonsorial artist.   la prima volta d'un barbitonsore.
I bravely will surrender to   Guidatemi al ridicolo
the outrage of the razor.   oltraggio d'un rasoio.

SCHAUNARD, COLLINE AND MARCELLO

    Let's go!   Andiam!

RODOLFO

    I stay here.   Io resto
I must complete the article   per terminar l'articolo
for my new journal 'The Beaver'.   del mio giornale: 'Il Castoro'.

MARCELLO

    Be quick, then.   Fa presto.

RODOLFO

Five minutes only. I've not much to do.   Cinque minuti. Conosco il mestiere.

COLLINE

We will await you at the porter's lodge.   Ti aspetterem dabbasso dal portiere.

MARCELLO

We'll shout if you don't hurry!   Se tardi, udrai che coro!

SCHAUNARD

You must shorten the Beaver's growing   Taglia corta la coda al tuo 'Castor'!
tale!

(Rodolfo takes a light from the table and opens the door; Marcello, Schaunard and Colline go out and descend the staircase.)

MARCELLO
(off-stage)

Look to the staircase! Keep well   Occhio alla scala. Tieni
to the handrail!   alla ringhiera.

61

RODOLFO
(still at the door, holding up the candle)

Go slowly!   Adagio!

COLLINE

Infernal darkness!   È buio pesto!

SCHAUNARD

May the porter be damned!   Maledetto portier!

(A crash off-stage, as though somebody has fallen down)

COLLINE

Devil take it!   Accidenti!

RODOLFO
(at the open door)

Colline, are you dead yet?   Colline, sei morto?

COLLINE
(from the bottom of the staircase)

Not just yet!   Non ancor!

MARCELLO
(further off)

Come quickly!   Vien presto!

Rodolfo — later Mimì

(Rodolfo shuts the door, puts the candle down, clears a corner of the table, takes pen and paper and, when he has blown out the other candle, he sits down to write; restless and lacking inspiration, he tears up the paper and throws down the pen.)

RODOLFO

No inspiration!   Non sono in vena.

(There is a timid knock at the door.)

Who's there?   Chi è là?

MIMI
(off-stage)

Excuse me.   Scusi.

RODOLFO

It's a lady!   Una donna!

MIMI
[10]

My candle, would you kindly   Di grazia, mi s'è spento
light it.   il lume.

RODOLFO
(running to open the door)

Surely.   Ecco.

MIMI
(standing at the door with a candle that has blown out and a key)

Oh, thank you.   Vorrebbe . . . ?

RODOLFO

Come in for just a moment.   S'accomodi un momento.

MIMI

No, I cannot.   Non occorre.

RODOLFO
(insistent)

I beg you, enter.   La prego, entri.

62

(Mimì enters, but she is seized by a fit of coughing.) [6]

RODOLFO
(concerned)

What is the matter?   Si sente male?

MIMI

It's nothing.   No ... nulla.

RODOLFO

You're pale and trembling!   Impallidisce!

MIMI
(still coughing)

I'm exhausted ... It's the staircase ...   È il respir ... Quelle scale ...

(She swoons, and Rodolfo has hardly time to support her and lower her onto a chair; she drops her candlestick and key.)

RODOLFO
(embarrassed)

What can I do to help her?   Ed ora come faccio? ...
        (He fetches some water and sprinkles it on her face.)
                    Ah! yes!   Cosi!
        (looking at her with great interest)
How very pale her face is!   Che viso d'ammalata!
                (She revives.)
        Do you feel better?   Si sente meglio?

MIMI
(almost in a whisper)

                    Yes!   Si.

RODOLFO

It is very chilly. Come near the fire, I beg   Qui c'è tanto freddo. Segga vicino al
you.   fuoco.
        (He helps Mimì to her feet and leads her to a chair nearer the stove.)
A moment ... a little wine.   Aspetti ... un po' di vino.
        (He runs over to the table and takes bottle and glass.)

MIMI

        Thank you!   Grazie.

RODOLFO
(He gives her the glass and pours out the wine.)

        For you.   A lei.

MIMI

        Not too much, please.   Poco, poco.

RODOLFO

Like this?   Cosi?

MIMI

        Thank you.   Grazie.

                (She drinks.)

RODOLFO
(admiring her)

        (So young and so lovely!)   (Che bella bambina!)

MIMI
(Rising, she looks for her candlestick.)

                    Now please allow me   Ora permetta
to light my candle. I'm feeling better.   che accenda il lume. È tutto passato.

RODOLFO

        Must you go now?   Tanta fretta?

63

Yes.   Sì.

(Rodolfo lights Mimì's candle and gives it to her without speaking,)

MIMI

Thank you. And good evening.   Grazie. Buona sera.

RODOLFO
(He accompanies her to the door, and returns to his table.)

Well, good evening.   Buona sera.

MIMI
(She goes out, then appears again in the doorway.)

               Oh! Oh! Heaven! [7]   Oh! sventata!
How dreadful! The key of my poor attic!   Sventata! La chiave della stanza!
Where can I have left it?   Dove l'ho lasciata?

RODOLFO

Come, don't stand in the doorway;   Non stia sull'uscio;
the draught will again put out your candle.   il lume vacilla al vento.

(Mimì's candle goes out.)

MIMI

Oh heaven! Light it again for me.   Oh Dio! Torni ad accenderlo.

RODOLFO
(He runs with his candle to light Mimì's, but his also blows out and the room is in darkness.)

Oh no! Mine has just gone out too!   Oh Dio! . . . anche il mio s'è spento.

MIMI

Ah! And they key, where can it be?   Ah! e la chiave ove sarà?

RODOLFO

Damn this darkness!   Buio pesto!

MIMI

               I'm so sorry!   Disgraziata!
(Groping about, she reaches the table and puts down the candlestick.)

RODOLFO

               Where can it be?   Ove sarà?

MIMI
(with cautious politeness)

Pray forgive your tiresome neighbour . . .   Importuna è la vicina . . .

RODOLFO

Nothing, I assure you!   Ma le pare!

MIMI

Pray forgive your tiresome neighbour . . .   Importuna è la vicina . . .

RODOLFO
(turning where he hears the voice)

It is nothing, I assure you!   Cosa dice, ma le pare!

(He finds himself near the door and closes it.)

MIMI

Look for it.   Cerchi.
(She looks for the key on the floor, sliding her feet over it. Rodolfo does the same and, finding the table, puts his candlestick on it. He resumes his search patting the floor with his hands.)

RODOLFO

I'm looking! Ah!   Cerco. Ah! . . .
(He finds the key and slips it into his pocket.)

MIMI

Have you found it?

RODOLFO

No.   No ...

MIMI

I thought so.   Mi parve ...

RODOLFO

I thought so too!   ... in verità!

(*Guided by Mimì's voice, Rodolfo pretends to search while drawing nearer to her. Mimì is kneeling on the floor feeling for her key. Rodolfo's hand meets Mimì's and he grasps it.*)

MIMI
(*surprised and rising suddenly*)

Ah!   Ah!

RODOLFO
(*holding Mimì's hand*)

Your tiny hand is frozen!	[8] Che gelida manina,
Let me warm it into life.	se la lasci riscaldar.
Our search is useless. In darkness all is hidden.	Cercar che giova? — Al buio non si trova.
But very soon now the moon will be shining, and in the moonlight our search we'll continue.	Ma per fortuna — è una notte di luna, e qui la luna l'abbiamo vicina.
I beg you stay a moment, while I tell you very briefly just who I am, what I do, and how I earn my living. Shall I?	Aspetti, signorina, e intanto le dirò con due parole chi son, chi son, e che faccio, e come vivo. Vuole?

(*Mimì is silent.*)

Now then, I am, but a poor poet. What's my vocation? Writing! Is that a living? Hardly!	Chi son? Chi son? Sono un poeta. Che cosa faccio? Scrivo. E come vivo? Vivo.
I'm poor but I am happy. Ladies of rank and fashion all inspire me with passion.	In povertà mia lieta. Scialo da gran signore rime ed inni d'amore.
In dreams and fond illusions or castles in the air ... richer is none on earth than I!	Per sogni, e per chimere e per castelli in aria ... l'anima ho milionaria.
Two lovely eyes have stolen every precious possession from my wealth of hidden treasures.	[9] Talor dal mio forziere ruban tutti i gioielli due ladri: gli occhi belli.
Your roguish eyes have robbed me, of all my dreams bereft me, dreams so fair yet so fleeting, fancies that are no more –	V'entrar con voi pur ora, ed i miei sogni usati ed i bei sogni miei, tosto si dileguar!
and yet I don't regret them. For now rosy morning is breaking and golden love awaking!	Ma il furto non m'accora, poichè vi ha preso stanza la dolce speranza!
Now you know all my story, pray tell me yours, too. Won't you tell me who you are? May I not know?	Or che mi conoscete, parlate voi. Deh! parlate. Chi siete? Vi piaccia dir?

MIMI
(*She hesitates a little, then decides to speak.*)

Yes.	Sì.
I'm always called Mimì, but my name is Lucia. My story is a short one. In my poor room	[10] Mi chiamano Mimì. ma il mio nome è Lucia. La storia mia è breve. A tela o a seta

I embroider silk and satin.	ricamo in casa e fuori . . .
I'm content and happy,	Son tranquilla e lieta
I love to fashion	ed è mio svago
the rose and lily.	far gigli e rose.
These flowers give me pleasure [11]	Mi piaccion quelle cose
as in magical accents	che han si dolce malia,
they speak to me of love, of	che parlano d'amor, di primavere, . . .
lovely springtime . . .	
of fancies and of visions bright they tell me me,	che parlano di sogni e di chimere,
such as poets, and only poets know . . .	quelle cose che han nome poesia . . .
Are you listening?	Lei m'intende?

RODOLFO
(*moved*)

Yes.	Si.

MIMI

I'm always called Mimì,	Mi chiamano Mimì.
but I know not why!	il perchè non so.
All by myself [12a]	Sola, mi fo
I have my frugal supper.	il pranzo da me stessa.
I go to mass but seldom	Non vado sempre a messa,
yet say my prayers each day.	ma prego assai il Signor.
I'm alone but not lonely.	Vivo sola, soletta,
There in my room so white and cosy	là in una bianca cameretta:
I look above me into the sky.	guardo sui tetti e in cielo;
Yet, when the frost is over,	ma quando vien lo sgelo
there first the sunlight greets me . . .	il primo sole è mio . . .
Spring's first awakening kiss is mine! . . .	il primo bacio dell'aprile è mio!
Her first bright sunbeam is mine!	il primo sole è mio!
How sweet is the rose that is opening, [11]	Germoglia in un vaso una rosa
every petal I cherish.	foglia a foglia la spio! . . .
Oh, what delight	Cosi gentil
is a flower in blossom!	il profumo d'un fior!
The flowers I fashion, alas! they have no perfume!	Ma i fior ch'io faccio, ahimè! non hanno odore!
More than just this I cannot find to tell you,	Altro di me non le saprei narrare.
I'm your tiresome neighbour	Sono la sua vicina
that at an awkward moment intrudes upon you.	che la vien fuori d'ora a importunare.

SCHAUNARD
(*from the courtyard*)

Hey there! Rodolfo!	Ehi! Rodolfo!

COLLINE

Rodolfo!	Rodolfo!

MARCELLO

Hallo! D'you hear us?	Olà. Non senti?

(*Rodolfo is annoyed at the shouts of his friends.*) [1]

Don't dawdle!	Lumaca!

COLLINE

Come on, scribbler!	Poetucolo!

SCHAUNARD

Hurry up there, idler!	Accidenti al pigro!

(*Getting more annoyed, Rodolfo goes to the window and opens it to answer his friends in the courtyard; from the open window a few rays of moonlight enter, brightening the room.*)

RODOLFO
(*at the window*)

I have still three lines to finish.	Scrivo ancor tre righe a volo.

MIMI
(approaching the window a little)

Who are they?	Chi sono?

RODOLFO

Companions.	Amici.

SCHAUNARD

What's all this delay?	Sentirai le tue.

MARCELLO

Why stay so long alone here?	Che te ne fai lì solo?

RODOLFO

I'm not lonely. There are two of us.	Non son solo. Siamo in due.
We'll meet you Chez Momus. Keep us two places,	Andate da Momus, tenete il posto,
we will follow quickly.	ci saremo tosto.

(He remains at the window to make sure his friends have gone.)

MARCELLO, SCHAUNARD AND COLLINE
(departing)

Momus, Momus, Momus,	Momus, Momus, Momus,
off to Momus discreetly we must go.	zitti e discreti andiamocene via.
Momus, Momus, Momus,	Momus, Momus, Momus,
and poetry will flow.	trovò la poesia.

(Mimì stands wreathed in moonlight near the window; turning, Rodolfo sees her and contemplates her in ecstasy.)

RODOLFO

Lovely maid in the moonlight, vision entrancing	O soave fanciulla, o dolce viso
enfolded in the radiance from above;	di mite circonfuso alba lunar,
with you before me	in te, ravviso
the dream that I would ever dream now returns!	il sogno ch'io vorrei sempre sognar!
Ah, my heart for evermore . . .	[9] Fremon già nell'anima . . .
bound by love's enchantment.	le dolcezze estreme.

MIMI

Ah, my heart for evermore . . .	Ah! tu sol commandi amor!
Ah, love's eternal enchantment . . .	tu sol commandi amore!

RODOLFO
(putting his arm around Mimì)

Love now shall rule our hearts	Fremon nell'anima
Now and forever lost in magic enchantment . . .	dolcezze estreme . . .

MIMI
(yielding to her lover's embrace)

Sweet to my soul the magic voice	Oh! come dolci scendono
of love its song is singing . . .	le sue lusinghe al core . . .

BOTH

Life's fairest flower is love!	Tu sol commandi amor!

(He kisses her.)

MIMI
(disengaging herself)

No, I beg you!	No, per pietà!

RODOLFO

I love you!	Sei mia!

MIMI

Your comrades await you.   V'aspettan gli amici . . .

RODOLFO

    Do you then dismiss me?   Già mi mandi via?

MIMI
(hesitating)

May I ask . . . no . . . I dare not . . .   Vorrei dir . . . ma non oso . . .

RODOLFO
(gently)

Say!   Di'!

MIMI
(coquettishly)

    Could I not come with you?   Se venissi con voi?

RODOLFO
(surprised)

    What? Mimi!   Che? . . . Mimi!
(suggestively)

It would be far more pleasant to stay here.   Sarebbe così dolce restar qui.
Outside it's chilly.   C'è freddo fuori.

MIMI

    I'll be always near you!   Vi starò vicina! . . .

RODOLFO

On returning?   E al ritorno?

MIMI
(archly)

    Who knows, sir?   Curioso!

RODOLFO

Take my arm, my little maiden.   [8] Dammi il braccio, mia piccina . . .

MIMI
(She gives her arm to Rodolfo.)

I obey you, my lord! . . .   Obbedisco, signor!

(They go arm in arm to the door.)

RODOLFO

Say you love me . . .   Che m'ami dì' . . .

MIMI
(with abandon)

    I love you.   Io t'amo!

(They go out.)

BOTH
(off-stage, gradually dying away)

    My love!   Amor!

Curtain.

... Gustave Colline, the great philosopher; Marcello, the great painter; Rodolfo, the great poet; and Schaunard, the great musician — as they were wont to style themselves — regularly frequented the Café Momus where, being inseparable, they were nicknamed the four musketeers.

Indeed they always went about together, played together, dined together, often without paying the bill, yet always with a beautiful harmony worthy of the Conservatoire Orchestra.

Mademoiselle Musetta was a pretty girl of twenty . . .

Very coquettish, rather ambitious, but without any pretensions to spelling.

Oh, those delightful suppers in the Quartier Latin!

A perpetual alternative between a blue brougham and an omnibus; between the Rue Breda and the Quartier Latin.

' Well, what of that? From time to time I feel the need of breathing the atmosphere of such a life as this. My madcap existence is like a song; each of my love-episodes forms a verse of it; but Marcello is its refrain.'

A scene from the 1977 ENO production designed by Hubert Monloup, with Lois McDonall as Musetta (photo: Donald Southern)

Act Two

In the Latin Quarter.

Christmas Eve. Streets converge on a square flanked by shops and traders of every kind; on one side, the Café Momus.

A vast, motley crowd; citizens, soldiers, serving-girls, boys, girls, children, students, seamstresses, gendarmes, etc..

Aloof from the crowd, Rodolfo and Mimì walk up and down; Colline is near a rag shop; Schaunard is buying a pipe and horn from a tinker. Marcello is being hustled hither and thither.

It is evening. The shops are decked with tiny lamps and lighted lanterns; a large lantern illuminates the entrance to the Café Momus. The Café is very crowded, and people are seated at a table outside. [13]

HAWKERS
(outside their shops)

Come, buy my oranges!	[14] Aranci, datteri!
Hot roasted chestnuts!	Caldi i marroni!
Trinkets and crosses!	Ninnoli, croci!
Fine hardbake!	Torroni!
Excellent toffee!	E caramelle!
Flowers for the ladies!	Fiori alle belle!
Try our candy!	La crostata!
Cream for the babies!	Panna montata!
Fat larks and ortolans!	Fringuelli, passeri!
Look at them!	Datteri!
Fine salmon!	Trote!
Chocolate! Candy!	Latte di cocco!
Who'll buy my carrots!	Giubbe! Carote!

TOWNSFOLK

What an uproar!	Quanta folla!

WOMEN

What an uproar!	Che chiasso!

STUDENTS AND SEAMSTRESSES

Hold fast to me! Come along!	Stringiti a me, corriamo!

TOWNSFOLK

Come, let us pass!	Date il passo!

MOTHER
(calling her child)

Emma! why don't you hear me!	Emma, quando ti chiamo!

CUSTOMERS AT THE CAFÉ MOMUS
(shouting to the waiters who run to and fro)

Come along! Come along!	Presto, qua, camerier!
Waiter!	Corri!
To me!	A me!
Waiter!	Birra!
With a beer!	Un bicchier!
Vanilla!	Vaniglia! . . .
Hurry up!	Ratafià!
Bring me a drink!	Dunque? Presto! . . .
A beer!	Da ber!
Some coffee!	Un caffè! . . .
Hurry up!	Presto, olà! . . .

(The crowd flows into the adjacent streets, people bustling in and out of the shops. In the Café Momus customers arrive and others depart, some going off in one direction, some in another. At the crossroads there is all the colour and excitement of a busy thoroughfare.)

SCHAUNARD
(He blows the horn, which emits strange notes.)

What a dreadful D! What a dreadful D!   Falso questo re!... Falso questo re!...
(haggling with the tinker)
And how much will it be?   Pipa e corno quant'è?...

(Arm in arm, Rodolfo and Mimì pass through the crowd making their way to the milliner's.)

RODOLFO

Let's go.   Andiam.

MIMI

Let's go and buy the bonnet.   Andiam per la cuffietta?

RODOLFO

Hold tightly to my arm, love.   Tieni al mio braccio stretta...

MIMI

To you I'm clinging. Let's go.   A te mi stringo. Andiam...
(They enter the milliner's.)

COLLINE
(to the clothes-dealer who is mending a coat he has just bought)

It's rather shabby,   È un poco usato,
but sound and not expensive!   ma è serio e a buon mercato...
(He pays and distributes his books equally in the many pockets of his great coat.)

MARCELLO
(alone in the midst of the crowd, with a parcel under his arm, ogling the girls by whom he is jostled)

I'm in the mood to shout and cry aloud.   Io pur mi sento in vena di gridare:
Ho, merry maidens, will you play at love?   chi vuol, donnine allegre, un po' d'amor?
Let's play together the game of buy and   Facciamo insieme a vendere e a comprar!...
sell!...
(accosting a girl)
Who'll give a penny for my virgin heart?   Io dò a un soldo il vergine mio cuor.

(The girl runs away, laughing.)

HAWKERS

Oranges! Salmon!   Datteri! Trote!

A HAWKER
(crossing the stage and shouting)

Who'll buy my plums?   Prugne di Tours!

SALESWOMEN

Buy our pretty scarf pins!   Ninnoli, spillette!
Try our toffee and our hardbake!   Datteri e caramelle!

SCHAUNARD
(He strolls about in front of the Café Momus waiting for his friends; and armed with his huge pipe and horn, he intently watches the crowd.)

Surging onward, swift and breathless,   Fra spintoni e pestate accorrendo affretta
moves the madding throng
as they seek the round of pleasure   la folla e si diletta
in their merry and maddening insane   nel provar gioie matte — insoddisfatte.
endeavour!

COLLINE
(He comes up to his friends wrapped up in his oversize great coat, which looks like a Roman toga, waving an old book in triumph.)

Such a rare book and quite unique,   Copia rara, anzi unica:
it's a volume of Runic rhyme.   la grammatica Runica!

SCHAUNARD
(looking pityingly over Colline's shoulder)

Honest fellow!   Uomo onesto! . . .

MARCELLO
(On reaching the Café, he shouts to Schaunard and Colline.)

To supper!   A cena!

SCHAUNARD AND COLLINE

Rodolfo?   Rodolfo?

MARCELLO

He's gone to buy a bonnet!   Entrò da una modista.

(Marcello, Shaunard and Colline enter the Café Momus, but leave almost immediately, disdaining the noisy crowd of people. They bring out a table and are followed by a waiter, who can well understand their desire to eat outside. The townsfolk at the neighbouring table, irritated by the din of the three friends, get up and leave. Meanwhile Rodolfo and Mimì come out of the milliner's.)

RODOLFO
(to Mimì)

Come along; my friends are waiting here.   Vieni, gli amici aspettano.

MIMI

Do you like this bonnet trimmed with   Mi sta ben questa cuffietta rosa?
roses?

RODOLFO

         The colour   Sei bruna
suits your complexion.   e quel color ti dona.

MIMI
(looking regretfully into the shop-window)

       That necklace   Bel vezzo
is so pretty!   di corallo!

RODOLFO

      I've an aunt,   Ho uno zio
a millionairess.   milionario.
When the good God wills to take her,   Se fa senno il buon Dio,
then I shall buy you many more like this.   voglio comprarti un vezzo assai più bel!

(They walk away talking together and are lost in the crowd. At a shop at the back, a shopman gesticulates frantically as he stands on a stool and offers underclothes, nightcaps, etc. for sale. Girls gather round his shop and laugh gaily.)

CITIZENS

Now let us follow the others!   Facciam coda alle gente!
Be careful, girls, be careful!   Ragazze, state attente!
Rue Mazarin's the nearest!   Pigliam via Mazzarino!
Let's get away, I'm choking!   Io soffoco, partiamo!
Let's go to the Café. Let's go to the   Vedi? il caffè è vicin! Andiam là da Momus!
'Momus'!

(Mimì and Rodolfo return. She notices a group of students.)

RODOLFO
(in a tone of playful remonstrance)

What is it?   Che guardi?

MIMI

Are you jealous?   Sei geloso?

RODOLFO

The man in love is always jealous.   All'uom felice sta il sospetto accanto.

MIMI

Then you love me?   Sei felice?

72

RODOLFO
(taking her under the arm)

Yes, I love you. And you?   Ah si, tanto. E tu?

MIMI

I love you.   Si, tanto.

(Mimì and Rodolfo join his friends.)

COLLINE

How I detest the vulgar crowd like Horace.   Odio il profano volgo al par d'Orazio.

SCHAUNARD

And when I'm eating,   Ed, io, quando mi sazio,
I can't stand being crowded.   vo' abbondanza di spazio.

MARCELLO
(to the waiter)

We want a supper of the choicest!   Vogliamo una cena prelibata.
Quickly!   Lesto!

SCHAUNARD

We're hungry.   Per molti.

MARCELLO, SCHAUNARD AND COLLINE

Quickly!   Lesto!

PARPIGNOL'S VOICE
(approaching from a distance)

Who'll buy some pretty toys from   Ecco i giocattoli di Parpignol!
Parpignol!

RODOLFO
(He arrives with Mimì.)

Two places.   Due posti.

COLLINE

So you've come then!   Finalmente?

RODOLFO

Yes, we are here.   Eccoci qui.
(He introduces Mimì)
This is Mimì,   Questa è Mimì,
our pretty neighbour.   gaia — fioraia.
Our party is completed,   Il suo venir completa
now she has come to join us,   la bella compagnia,
for though I am the poet,   perchè son io il poeta,
she is my inspiration.   essa la poesia.
Forth from my mind poems are flowing,   Dal mio cervel sbocciano i canti,
lilies and roses bloom at her touch ... dalle sue dita sbocciano i fior;
and in our souls awakens   dall'anime esultanti
beautiful Love!   sboccia l'amor!

(Marcello, Schaunard and Colline laugh.)

MARCELLO
(sarcastically)

Heavens! What lofty concepts!   Dio, che concetti rari!

COLLINE
(with a grave bow to Mimì)

'Digna est intrari.'   'Digna est intrari.'

SCHAUNARD
(with mock dignity)

'Ingrediat si necessit.'   'Ingrediat si necessit.'

I'll grant only an   Io non dò che un

accessit!   accessit.

(*Rodolfo beckons Mimì to be seated; they all sit down; the waiter returns with the menu. To the waiter*)

Hey stupid!   Salame ...

(*The waiter presents the menu to the four companions who pass it round, each studying its impressive contents carefully. Enter Parpignol from the Rue Dauphin, pushing a barrow festooned with foliage, flowers and paper lanterns.*)

PARPIGNOL
(*shouting*)

Who'll buy some pretty toys from   Ecco i giocattoli di Parpignol!
   Parpignol!

(*He is surrounded by a crowd of merry urchins.*)

BOYS AND GIRLS

Parpignol! Parpignol!   Parpignol! Parpignol!
With his pretty barrow bright with flowers.   Col ... carretto ... tutto fior!
                          (*ogling the toys*)
I want the drum, and I the horse.   Voglio la tromba, il cavallin!
No, the drum shall be mine.   Il tambur, tamburel,
I want the gun, and I the whip.   Voglio il cannon, voglio il frustin!
Well you can't, I was first.   dei soldati il drappel.

(*At the shrieks of the children, their scolding mothers approach to tear them away from Parpignol.*)

MOTHERS

Ah! Get away, you dirty little rascals!   Ah! razza di furfanti indemoniati,
What can it be that sets you all agaping?   che ci venite a fare in questo loco?
Get home to your beds, you wicked rascals,   A casa! A letto! Via, brutti sguaiati.
or you shall all have such a painful beating!   Gli scappelloti vi parranno poco! ...

A BOY
(*whimpering*)

Want a trumpet! Want a drum!   Vo' la tromba, il cavallin!

(*The mothers relent and buy the toys, to the intense delight of the children. Parpignol turns into Rue Vieille Comédie, pursued by children banging drums and blowing trumpets.*)

PARPIGNOL
(*from far off*)

Who'll buy some pretty toys from Parpignol!   Ecco i giocattoli di Parpignol!

BOYS AND GIRLS
(*following him off, their shouts receding in the distance*)

Long live Parpignol, Parpignol!   Viva Parpignol, Parpignol!
Buy the drum, buy the drum!   Il tambur, tamburel,
Get away it is mine!   dei soldati il drappel!

(*Meanwhile the friends have been ordering their meal.*)

SCHAUNARD
(*to the waiter*)

Bring some mutton.   Cervo arrosto.

MARCELLO

I'll have turkey.   Un tacchino.

SCHAUNARD

And some Rhenish! And some lobster, only   Vin del Reno! Aragosta senza crosta!
   shell it!

COLLINE

Bring some burgundy!   Vin da tavola!

RODOLFO
(to Mimì, softly)

Mimi, what would you like?	E tu, Mimì, che vuoi?

MIMI

Some ice cream.	La crema.

SCHAUNARD

Great occasion. She's a lady!	È gran sfarzo. C'è una dama!

MARCELLO
(to Mimì, with politeness)

Will you tell us Mimì, what loving present did you receive from Rodolfo?	Signorina Mimì, che dono raro le ha fatto il suo Rodolfo?

MIMI

This little bonnet trimmed with lace and roses, very pretty, do you not think it suits my fair complexion? So many times I've set my very heart on such a bonnet! . . . and he discovered what my heart had longed for . . . Now one who reads the heart's long hidden secrets is a master, a mighty master.	Una cuffietta a pizzi, tutta rosa, ricamata; coi miei capelli bruni ben si fonde. Da tanto tempo tal cuffietta è cosa desïata! . . . Ed egli ha letto quel che il core asconde . . . Ora colui che legge dentro a un cuore sa l'amore ed è . . . lettore.

SCHAUNARD

A very great professor . . .	Esperto professore . . .

COLLINE
(taking up Schaunard's idea)

. . . already qualified, though less in verse than other matters.	. . . che ha già diplomi e non son armi prime le sue rime . . .

SCHAUNARD
(interrupting him)

. . . all the poetic tales seem to have meaning.	. . . tanto che sembra ver ciò ch'egli esprime!

MARCELLO
(looking at Mimì)

Oh sweetest dreams of hope and lover's fancies you trust, you hope and all seems fair and splendid.	O bella età d'inganni e d'utopie! Si crede, spera, e tutto bello appare!

RODOLFO

My friend, the most divine of all our poems is that which truly teaches us to love.	La più divina delle poesie è quella, amico che c'insegna amare!

MIMI

And surely love is sweeter far than honey.	Amare è dolce ancora più del miele . . .

MARCELLO
(vexed)

According to taste it's honey or vinegar.	. . . secondo il palato è miele, o fiele! . . .

MIMI
(to Rodolfo, surprised)

Oh Heavens! I have hurt him.	O Dio! . . . l'ho offeso!

RODOLFO

He's mourning, my Mimì.	È in lutto, o mia Mimì . . .

SCHAUNARD AND COLLINE
(*changing the subject*)

·Now let's have a toast.	Allegri, o un toast!

MARCELLO

Give me some more.	Qua del liquor!

MIMI, RODOLFO AND MARCELLO
(*while all get up*)

Let's drown our	E via i pensier!
sorrow with more wine!	Alti i bicchier!

ALL

Let's drink! . . . Let's drink!	Beviam! . . . beviam! . . .

MARCELLO
(*breaking off as he sees Musetta in the distance*)

Bring me a bottle of poison!	Ch'o beva del tossico!

(*From the corner of the Rue Mazarin appears an extremely pretty, coquettish-looking young lady. She is followed by a pompous old gentleman, who is both fussy and overdressed. On seeing her friends round the table, she stops, as if finding what she had come for.*) [16]

RODOLFO, SCHAUNARD AND COLLINE
(*surprised to see Musetta*)

Oh! Musetta! She's here!	Oh! Musetta! Essa!

(*Their eyes full of compassion, Marcello's friends look at their companion who has gone pale. The waiter serves them. Schaunard and Colline continue to keep an eye on Musetta and talk about her. Marcello pretends indifference. Only Rodolfo cannot take his eyes and mind off Mimì.*)

SHOP-WOMEN
(*As they are about to disappear they linger a moment outside their shops to stare at the finely-dressed lady; they are surprised to recognise Musetta and whisper among themselves as they point to her*)

Look! It's Musetta!	To', è Musetta!
Her!	Lei!
Musetta!	Tornata.
Yes.	Sì.
Yes.	Sì.
Oh! What a swagger!	Siamo in auge!
My! She's gorgeous!	Che toeletta!

(*They enter their shops.*)

ALCINDORO DE MITONNEAUX
(*catching up with Musetta, breathless*)

Just like a valet	Come un facchino
I must run here . . . and there . . .	correr di qua . . . di là . . .
No! Not for me . . .	No! Non ci stà . . .
I can stand no more!	Io non ne posso più!

MUSETTA

Come, Lulù!	Vien, Lulù!

(*Ignoring Alcindoro, she makes her way towards the Café Momus and occupies the vacated table.*)

SCHAUNARD

He's had a pretty good time, I reckon.	Quel brotto coso mi par che sudi!

ALCINDORO

What's that,	Come!
outside here?	Qui fuori!? Qui!?

MUSETTA
(*paying no heed to the protests of Alcindoro, who is terrified of staying out in the cold*)

Sit here, Lulù!	Siedi, Lulù!

(*Alcindoro, in a state of great irritation, sits down and turns up his coat collar.*)

ALCINDORO
(grumbling)

Do not employ these endearments in public, for heaven's sake.	Tali nomignoli, prego, serbateli al tu per tu.

(A waiter approaches to lay the table.)

MUSETTA

Now don't be such a prude.	Non farmi il Barbablù!

COLLINE
(scrutinising Alcindoro)

The naughty, naughty Elder!	È il vizio conte gnoso ...

MARCELLO
(contemptuously)

With his virgin Susanna!	Colla casta Susanna!

MIMI
(to Rodolfo)

And her clothes are lovely.	È pur ben vestita.

RODOLFO

Angels are always naked.	Gli angeli vanno nudi.

MIMI
(to Rodolfo, with curiosity)

Do you know who she is?	La conosci? Chi è?

MARCELLO

You had better ask me.
  Her first name is Musetta;
  Her surname is Temptation!
  As to her vocation,
  like a reed in the breezes,
  she will vary her love
  and her lovers without number.
  And – like the spiteful raven,
  a bird that's most rapacious –
  and the food that she favours?
  The heart! Bloodthirsty raven!
  She's drained my heart of blood.
	Domandatelo a me.
	  Il suo nome è Musetta;
	  cognome: Tentazione!
	  Per sua vocazione
	  fa la rosa dei venti;
	  gira e muta soventi
	  d'amanti e d'amore,
	  e come la civetta
	  è uccello sanguinario;
	  il suo cibo ordinario
	  è il cuore!... Mangia il cuore!...
	  Per questo io non ne ho più ...

(to his friends, trying to hide the emotion getting the better of him)

So pass the turkey pie!	Passatemi il ragù!

MUSETTA
(disconcerted that her friends are not looking at her)

(Marcello must have seen me ... but he's not looking, the villain. That Schaunard is laughing! I can bear them no longer!	(Marcello ... mi vide ... e non mi guarda, il vile! Quel Schaunard che ride! Mi fan tutti una bile!

(Her irritation increases.)

They will see how I fight, if they push me too far! But meanwhile here I sit with this doddering fool. We'll see now!)	Se potessi picchiar, se potessi graffiar! Ma non ho sotto man che questo pellican! Aspetta!)

(She calls the waiter back.)

Waiter, come here!	Ehi! Camerier!

(When the waiter arrives, Musetta takes a plate and sniffs it.)

Waiter, come here! See this plate has a horrid smell of onions!	Ehi! Cameriere! Questo piatto ha una puzza di rifritto!

(She dashes the plate to the ground; the waiter picks up the pieces.)

(trying to calm her down)

No, Musetta, do be quiet!   No. Musetta . . . zitto, zitto!
Watch your manners!   Modi, garbo!

MUSETTA
(angry and still looking at Marcello)

(He won't look here. How I could beat him!)   (Non si volta. Ora lo batto!)

ALCINDORO

What's the matter?   Con chi parli? . . .

MUSETTA
(pettishly)

I meant the waiter! Hold your tongue!   Al cameriere! Non seccar!
Leave me alone! I do just what I please!   Voglia fare il mio piacere,
I won't be ruled by you, sir!   vo' far quel che mi pare!
What a bore! Ah!   Non seccar! Ah!

ALCINDORO

Not so loud, not so loud!   Parla pian, parla pian!

COLLINE

Oh! This chicken is tasty!   Questo pollo è un poema!

SCHAUNARD

This wine is most delicious!   Il vino è prelibato!

WORKGIRLS

Only look! Why there she is,   Guarda, guarda chi si vede,
Why there she is, Musetta!   proprio lei, Musetta!
Ha! ha!   Ah! Ah!

STUDENTS

Some old man is dining with her;   Con quel vecchio che balbetta
Why there she is, Musetta!   proprio lei, Musetta!
Ha! Ha!   Ah! Ah!

MUSETTA

(Can he be jealous of this old mummy?   (Che sia geloso di questa mummia?
But wait! I'll be even, see if I don't   Vediam se mi resta tanto poter
I'll pay him back, I'll pay him back!)   su lui da farlo cedere!)

ALCINDORO
(leaving the order, and trying to pacify Musetta)

What strange behaviour . . . be quiet!   La convenienza . . . il grado . . . la virtù . . .
   Do be calm!

SCHAUNARD
(to Colline)

This is surely the last act . . .   La commedia è stupenda!

MUSETTA
(looking towards Marcello, in a loud voice)

Why don't you look at me?   Tu non mi guardi!

ALCINDORO
(believing these words to be addressed to him)

I am giving the order, dear!   Vedi bene che ordino!

SCHAUNARD

. . . and this act is stupendous!   La commedia è stupenda!

COLLINE

Stupendous!   Stupenda!

SCHAUNARD
(to Colline)

To one she speaks because
the other listens.

Essa all'un parla
perchè l'altro intenda.

RODOLFO
(to Mimì)

I never could forgive you if
you behaved that way to me, my darling.

Sappi per tuo governo che
non darei perdono in sempiterno.

MIMI
(to Rodolfo)

I love you fondly, and I am yours forever.
Why then talk about forgiveness?

Io t'amo tanto, e sono tutta tua!
Che mi parli di perdono?

COLLINE
(to Schaunard)

The other will not hear,
feigns not to see the girl:
which makes her mad!

E l'altro invan crudel ...
finge di non capir,
ma sugge miel!

MUSETTA
(to herself)

But your heart is a-throbbing!

Ma il tuo cuore martella!

ALCINDORO

Do be quiet!

Parla piano!

MUSETTA
(coquettishly, turning towards Marcello, who shows signs of agitation)

As through the street I wander on my way [17]
the people turn to look at me.
My beauty fascinates them, all eyes admire
my grace and my charm.

Quando me'n vo' soletta per la via
la gente sosta e mira,
e la bellezza mia – tutta ricerca in me
da capo a piè.

MARCELLO
(to his friends in a voice half-choked with emotion)

Just tie me to this chair of mine!

Legatemi alla seggiola!

ALCINDORO
(in an agony of embarrassment)

What will all the people say?

Quella gente che dirà?

MUSETTA

And with delight I sense their silent vows
of love and the message of their glances
and then the joy of conquest fills my heart.
Every man is my prize.

Ed assaporo allor la bramosia
sottil, che da gl'occhi traspira
e dai palesi vezzi intender sa
alle occulte beltà.

(rising)

And thus their hearts, their hearts, I
  capture by magic –
what rapture is mine!

Così l'effluvio del desio tutta m'aggira

felice mi fa!

ALCINDORO
(trying to stop Musetta singing)

This odious singing upsets me
  entirely!

Quel canto scurrile mi muove
  la bile!

MUSETTA

All you that cherish the passion that
  betrayed you,
Why should this have dismayed you?
I know deep in your heart you'd never tell,
but would far rather die.

E tu che sai, che memori e ti struggi

da me tanto rifuggi?
So ben: le angoscie tue non le vuoi dir,
ma ti senti morir.

MIMI
(to Rodolfo)

I see that this unhappy girl here our friend Marcello!	Io vedo ben che quella poveretta tutta invaghita ell'è di Marcello!

RODOLFO

Marcello did love her once, then she left him without a word, rarer game she thought to capture.	Marcello un dì l'amò, la fraschetta l'abbandonò per poi darsi a miglior vita.

MIMI

I feel compassion for her unhappy life. Darling!	Quell'infelice mi muove a pietà. T'amo!

RODOLFO

Mimi!	Mimi!

MIMI

Yes, that poor girl fills my heart with sorrow! The love that's born of passion ends in despair!	Quell'infelice mi muove a pietà! L'amor ingeneroso è tristo amor.

RODOLFO

Most faint the love that, when it's wounded, may not make reply! None can revive a love that is dead!	È fiacco amor quel che le offese vendicar non sa! Non risorge spento amor!

COLLINE

Who knows what will happen now! From the tempting wiles of females I will always run away.	Chi sa mai quel che avverrà! Santi numi, in simil briga mai Colline intopperà.
(She is pretty, I don't doubt it, but yet I'd rather smoke my old pipe and read some Homer!)	(Essa è bella, io non son cieco, ma piaccionmi assai più una pipa e un testo greco.)

SCHAUNARD

Ah! Marcel will soon give in! But the snare to some is pleasant to the hunter and the prey. See the braggart in a moment will give in! The fun grows fast and furious!	Ah! Marcello cederia! trovan dolce a pari il laccio chi lo tende e chi ci dà. Quel bravaccio a momenti cederà! Stupenda è la commedia!

(to Colline)

If such a pretty damsel should but make an eye at you, you'd forget your mouldy classics and you'd run to fetch her shoe.	Se tal vaga persona ti trattasse a tu per tu, la tua scienza brontolona manderesti a Belzebù.

MUSETTA

Ah! Marcello, you're vanquished! Marcello you're vanquished. And though your heart is breaking you'd never let us know! Ah! you would never let us know.	Ah! Marcello smania, Marcello è vinto! So ben: le angoscie tue non le vuoi dir. Ah! ma ti senti morir.

(obstinately, to Alcindoro)

I'll have my way, so don't you worry! I will do just what I like, So hold your tongue. (I must try to get rid of the old boy.)	Io voglio fare il mio piacere! Voglio far quel che mi par non seccar, non seccar. (Or convien liberarsi del vecchio!)

(pretending to be in great pain)

Oh!	Ahi!

ALCINDORO

What now?	Che c'è?

(pretending to suffer violent pain in her foot, she sits down again)

How it's aching, it's burning! Qual dolore, qual bruciore!

ALCINDORO

What is? Dove?

MUSETTA
(coyly showing her foot)

My foot! Al piè!
(shrieking)

Break it! Tear it! I can't bear it!	Sciogli, slaccia, rompi, straccia!
Do, I beg you!	te ne imploro!
Close by there is a bootshop!	Laggiù c'è un calzolaio.
Hasten, quickly!	Corri, presto!

ALCINDORO
(trying to untie her shoe)

What imprudence! Imprudente!

MUSETTA

He may have boots to please me, Ne voglio un altro paio.
Ah! The torture! How these Ahi! Che fitta, maledetta
horrid tight shoes squeeze me! Scarpa stretta!
I'll not wear them. Or la levo ...

ALCINDORO
(outraged)

What will all the people say? Quella gente che dirà?
What impudence! Ma il mio grado!

MUSETTA
(She takes off her shoe and puts it on the table.)

So there they are! Hurry! Go! Hurry! Eccola qua. Corri, va, corri!
Say no more! Go! Presto, va! va!

ALCINDORO

Nothing short of scandal! Vuoi ch'io comprometta?
Musetta! Shame! Aspetta! Musetta! Vo'.

MARCELLO
(greatly moved)

(Ah, happy memories, not yet have you (Gioventù mia tu non sei morta
    vanished
and nor have I forgotten you ... nè di te morto è il sovvenir ...
if at my door you came to greet me se tu battessi alla mia porta
my heart would go out to you my love!) t'andrebbe il mio core ad aprir!)

(As soon as Alcindoro is out of sight, Musetta gets up and throws her arms around Marcello, who shows equal fervour.) [17]

MUSETTA

Marcello! Marcello!

MARCELLO

Enchantress! Sirena!

SCHAUNARD

We have reached the finale! Siamo all'ultima scena!
(A waiter brings the bill.)

ALL
(except Marcello; in amazement)

The bill! Il conto!

SCHAUNARD

Why the hurry? Cosi presto?

81

Who had him bring it?   Chi l'ha richiesto?

SCHAUNARD
(to the waiter)

Let's see.   Vediam.

(He takes the bill, and then passes it round. The Tattoo, a band of the National Guard, is heard approaching in the distance.)

RODOLFO AND COLLINE

Heaven!   Caro!

COLLINE, SCHAUNARD AND RODOLFO

Out with your coppers!   Fuori il danaro!

SCHAUNARD

Colline, Rodolfo and you,   Colline, Rodolfo e tu
Marcello.   Marcel.

MARCELLO

We have no money!   Siamo all'asciutto!

SCHAUNARD

What's that?   Come?

RODOLFO

I've thirty sous, in total.   Ho trenta soldi in tutto!

MARCELLO, SCHAUNARD AND COLLINE

Really. No more than that?   Come? Non ce n'è più?

(As the military band is still a long way off people run hither and thither, as if uncertain from which direction it will arrive.) [18]

CITIZENS

Here come the soldiers!   La ritirata! La ritirata!

URCHINS

Will they come along this way?   S'avvicinan per di qua!?

CITIZENS

No, from there!   No, di là!

URCHINS
(pointing uncertainly the other way)

They are coming down this way!   S'avvicinan per di la!
Yes, here they come!   No, vien di la!

(Windows open, and mothers and children eagerly lean out waiting for the band.)

CITIZENS
(running forward)

Here they come!   Vien di qua!
Make way there!   Largo! Largo!

CHILDREN
(from the windows)

Just let me see! Just let me hear!   Voglio veder! Voglio sentir!

MOTHERS

Lisetta, do be quiet!   Lisetta, vuoi tacer!
Tony, do have done!   Tonio, la vuoi finir!

CHILDREN

Mama, just let me see,   Mamma, voglio veder!
Papa, just let me hear,   Papa, voglio sentir!
Now it's coming, the parade!   Vuò veder la ritirata!

In that parade you see our great country's noble might!	In quel rullio tu senti la patria maestà!

(Meanwhile, at the café table . . .)

SCHAUNARD
(sternly)

But where's my treasure gone?	Ma il mio tesoro ov'è?

(They all feel in their pockets, which are empty; none can explain the sudden disappearance of Schaunard's purse; they look at each other in surprise.)

MUSETTA

And the bill, give it to me.	Il mio conto date a me.

(to the waiter who brings it)

Thank you! Now will you make one bill of the two.	Bene! Presto sommate quello con questo . . .
You will be paid by the man who came with me!	Paga il signor che stava qui con me!

RODOLFO, MARCELLO, SCHAUNARD, COLLINE
(pointing to where Alcindoro went out, comically)

Yes, he will pay!	Paga il signor!

(putting the two bills together at Alcindoro's place)

When he returns he'll find this token of my admiration.	E dove s'è seduto ritrovi il mio saluto!

URCHINS

Now look out they're coming here! Make way there!	Ohè! attenti, eccoli qua! in fila!

CITIZENS

Do stand back, for here they come! Make way there!	Largo, largo, eccoli qua! in fila!

RODOLFO, MARCELLO, SCHAUNARD, COLLINE

See, the patrol is coming! Be careful the old boy doesn't catch you with his darling. Now the crowd is tremendous, to dodge him will be easy! Quickly, quickly, quickly! Long live Musetta, never let us down, Queen of our hearts, the Latin Quarter hails its glorious queen!	Giunge la ritirata; Che il vecchio non ci veda fuggir colla sua preda. Quella folla serrata il nascondiglio appresti! . . . Lesti, lesti, lesti! . . . Viva Musetta! Cuor birichin . . . Gloria ed onor del quartier latin!

(The patrol enters, headed by a gigantic drum-major and crosses the stage.)

THE CROWD

And there's the drum-major, as proudly a warrior of old they go marching by! Look at the drums go by! The drummers marching by! See! There he goes, the tall drum-major bold. The staff of gold you see him hold, he proudly twists and turns! See there he goes! The greatest man in France, The tall drum-major bold! The staff of gold he proudly twists and turns!	Ecco il tambur maggior, più fier d'un antico guerrier! Il tambur maggior! I Zappator olà! La ritirata è qua! Eccolo là! Il bel tambur maggior! La canna d'or, tutto splendor! Che guarda, passa, va! Tutto splendor! Di Francia è il più bell'uom! Il bel tambur maggior! Eccolo là! Che guarda, passa, va!

(Unable to walk with only one shoe, Musetta is carried aloft by Marcello and Colline; the crowd, seeing her carried triumphantly, cheer and applaud in agreement. Marcello and Colline with Musetta join the crowd following the soldiers; Rodolfo and Mimì walk behind arm in arm;

Schauard follows blowing on his horn. Students and seamstresses dance with joy, and behind them come boys, citizens and women. All make their way behind the military band singing. Alcindoro returns to the Café Momus with a parcel of shoes and searches for Musetta. He approaches the now deserted table and the waiter ceremoniously hands him the bills left behind by Musetta. Seeing the amount and no one left to pay it Alcindoro falls back on a chair defeated.)

(Curtain.)

A page from Puccini's manuscript score of Act Two (© Ricordi)

Mimì's voice seemed to go through Rodolfo's heart like a death knell . . .
His love for her was a jealous, fantastic, weird, hysterical love . . . Scores of
times they were on the point of separating. It must be admitted that their
existence was a veritable hell-upon-earth. And yet amid all their
tempestuous strife they mutually agreed to pause for the refreshment and
solace afforded by a night of love; but the dawn merely brought with it some
unlooked-for battle which served to drive Love, terrorstruck, away. Thus
(if life it was) did they live; a few happy days alternating with many
wretched ones while perpetually awaiting a divorce . . .

Either as a congenital defect or as a natural instinct, Musetta possessed a
positive genius for elegance.
Even in her cradle this strange creature must surely have asked for a
mirror.
Intelligent, shrewd, and above all hostile to anything that she considered
tyranny, she had but one rule, caprice.
In truth the only man that she really loved was Marcello; perhaps because
he alone could make her suffer. Yet extravagance was for her one of the
conditions of well-being.

A scene from the first performance in Turin in 1896.

Act Three

The Barrière d'Enfer.

*Beyond the toll-gate, the outer boulevard is formed in the background by the Orleans road,
half hidden by tall houses and the misty gloom of February. To the left is a tavern with a small
open space in front of the toll-gate. To the right is the Boulevard d'Enfer; to the left that of St
Jacques. On the right also there is the entrance to the Rue d'Enfer, leading to the Quartier
Latin.*
*Over the tavern, as its sign-board, hangs Marcello's picture 'The Passage of the Red Sea',
while underneath in large letters is the inscription 'At the Port of Marseilles'. On either side of
the door are frescoes of a Turk and a Zouave with a huge laurel leaf round his fez.*
*From the ground-floor windows of the tavern facing the toll-gate, light gleams. The plane-
trees, grey and gaunt, which flank the toll-gate square lead diagonally towards the two
boulevards. Between each tree is a marble bench. It is towards the close of February; snow
covers all.*

*As the curtain rises the scene is merged in the dim light of early dawn. In front of a brazier are
seated, in a group, snoring custom-house officers. From the tavern at intervals one may hear
laughter, shouts, and the clink of glasses. A custom-house officer comes out of the tavern with
wine. The toll-gate is closed. Behind the toll-gate, stamping their feet and blowing on their
frost-bitten fingers, stand several street-scavengers.* [19]

SCAVENGERS

Hallo! You soldiers! Admit us! Wake up!   Ohè, là, le guardie! . . . Aprite! . . . Ohè là!
Be quick and let us pass! . . . We are the   Quelli di Gentilly! . . . Siam gli spazzini!
sweepers!

*(The officers do not budge; so the scavengers with brooms and mattocks thump the toll-gate
and shout.)*

It's very cold here. We are frozen!   Fiocca la neve! . . . Qui s'agghiaccia!

(The officers wake up.)

AN OFFICER
(grumpily, yawning and stretching himself)

Coming!   Vengo!
*(He goes to open the gate; the scavengers pass through to the Rue d'Enfer. The officer closes the
gate again. From the tavern can be heard voices and the clink of glasses, forming an accompaniment to the song.)*

VOICES FROM WITHIN

Fill the glass! Each toast his love.   [20] Chi nel ber trovò il piacer,
So fill the glass! Let each lad toast his love!   nel suo bicchier, nel suo bicchier! Aa!
Ha!
Each one, as he drinks his wine,   D'una bocca nell'ardor,
Shall dream of lips made for love divine!   trovò l'amor, trovò l'amor!
Tralleralle, tralleralle, tralleralle . . .   Tralleralle, tralleralle, Eva e Noè!

MUSETTA
(from the tavern)

Ah! The drinker loves his glass,   [17] Ah! Se nel bicchiere sta il piacer
the lover loves his lass!   in giovin bocca sta l'amor!

*(A tinkling of bells is heard from the Orleans road: they are carts drawn by mules. The shouts
of the carters and the crack of whips can be heard. Between the wheels of the carts are lighted
lanterns. They pass along the outer boulevard.)*

VOICES
(from the outer boulevard)

Houp-là! Houp-là!   Hopp-là! Hopp-là!

OFFICERS

The vendors for the market place!   Son già le lattivendole!

(The Sergeant comes out of the guard-house and orders the toll-gate to be opened. Gloom gradually gives way to daylight.)

MILK-WOMEN
(They pass through the gate astride mules and take various roads, saying to the officers:)

Good morning!   Buon giorno!

(It stops snowing.)

PEASANT-WOMEN
(with baskets on their arms)

Cheese and butter!   Burro e cacio!
Eggs and poultry!   Polli ed ova!
(They pay the officials, who let them pass. At the crossroads:)
Which way, then, are you going?   Voi da che parte andate?
St Michael's Market.   A San Michele!
And shall we see you later?   Ci troverem più tardi?
At half-past twelve!   A mezzodì!

(They move off in various directions. The officers remove the bench and the brazier. Enter Mimì from the Rue d'Enfer [10]; she looks about her as if anxious to make sure of her whereabouts. As she reaches the first plane-tree, she is seized by a violent fit of coughing. Then, recovering herself, she sees the Sergeant and approaches him.)

MIMI
(to the Sergeant)

Oh, please sir, tell me, do you know the   Sa dirmi, scusi, qual'è l'osteria ...
    tavern ...
(unable to recollect the name)
where a painter is working?   dove un pittor lavora?

SERGEANT
(pointing to the tavern)

There it is.   Eccola.

MIMI

Thank you.   Grazie.

(A serving-woman comes out of the tavern.)

Oh! my good woman, pray do me this   O buona donna, mi fate il favore ...
    favour!
Can you find me the painter,   di cercarmi il pittore
Marcello? I wish to see him! The matter's   Marcello? Ho da parlargli. Ho tanta fretta.
    urgent!
Just tell him softly that Mimì is waiting.   Ditegli, piano, che Mimì l'aspetta.

(The serving-woman goes back into the tavern.)

SERGEANT
(to a passer-by)

Eh, in that basket!   Ehi, quel paniere!

OFFICERS

Empty!   Vuoto!

SERGEANT

Pass there!   Passi.

(Other folk pass through the toll-gate and move off in different directions. The bell of the Hospice Sainte Thérèse rings for matins. Day has now come; a sad, murky winter's day; sundry couples, homeward bound, quit the tavern.)

Marcello — Mimì

MARCELLO [1]
(Coming out of the inn, he is amazed to see Mimì.)

Mimì?!   Mimì?!

MIMI	
I hoped that I should find you here.	Speravo di trovarvi qui.
MARCELLO	
Yes, here we've been for a month;	È ver. Siam qui da un mese
so, to pay for our lodging,	di quell'oste alle spese.
Musetta teaches singing to those who come here;	Musetta insegna il canto ai passeggieri;
And I, I paint these warriors	io pingo quei guerrieri
here on the house-front.	sulla facciata.

(Mimì coughs.) [6]

It's cold here. Come in now.   È freddo. Entrate.

MIMI	
Where's C'è	
Rodolfo? Rodolfo?	

MARCELLO	
Here. Sì.	

MIMI
(bursting into tears)

I cannot go inside.   Non posso entrar, no, no!

MARCELLO
(surprised)

Why not?   Perchè?

MIMI
(in despair)

Ah! Good Marcello! Help me!   Oh! buon Marcello, aiuto!

MARCELLO	
Tell me what happened!	Cos'è avvenuto?

MIMI	
Rodolfo loves me, yet shuns me!	[21] Rodolfo m'ama e mi fugge,
My own dear lover is jealous, madly jealous . . .	il mio Rodolfo si strugge per gelosia, per gelosia . . .
A glance, a gesture,	Un passo, un detto,
a gift or flower will rouse in him suspicion,	Un vezzo, un fior lo mettono in sospetto . . .
waking his wrath and anger.	Onde corrucci ed ire.
And then at night, pretending to be sleeping,	Talor la notte fingo di dormire
I feel his eyes are watching,	e in me lo sento fiso
to spy upon my slumbers.	spiarmi i sogni in viso.
He cries at every moment:	Mi grida ad ogni 'stante:
'You're not for me. Go find another lover.'	'Non fai per me, ti prendi un altro amante!'
I cannot bear it.	Ahimè! Ahimè!
It's jealousy that drives him,	In lui parla il rovello,
I know; what can I say to him, Marcello?	lo so, ma che rispondergli, Marcello?

MARCELLO	
It would surely be better	Quando s'è come voi,
if you did not live together.	non si vive in compagnia.
I'm happy with Musetta, and she's happy with me, it's joy that binds us both together . . .	Son lieve a Musetta ell'è lieve a me, perchè ci amiamo in allegria . . .
Laughter, music and song	Canti e risa, ecco il fior
are the flowers of our love.	d'invariabile amor!

MIMI	
You are right, much better to leave him.	Dite bene. Lasciarci conviene.
Will you help us to part? So many times we have tried it. But in vain! . . .	Aiutateci voi? noi s'è provato più volte, ma invano!
Ah, then help us, I pray you!	Fate voi per il meglio.

88

MARCELLO

All right, I'll try! I'll go and wake him.　　　Sta bene, sta ben! Ora lo sveglio.

MIMÌ

Wake him?　　　Dorme?

MARCELLO

　　He came back just before　　　　　　　È piombato qui
the day was breaking, fell asleep　　　un'ora avanti l'alba s'assopi
upon a bench there.　　　　　　　　　sopra una panca.
　　　(motioning Mimì to look through the window)
　　　　　You see him.　　　　　　　　　　Guardate.
　　　　　　(Mimì coughs persistently.)
　　　　What coughing!　　　　　　　　　Che tosse!

MIMÌ

Unceasingly it shakes me.　　　　　Da ieri ho l'ossa rotte.
Last evening Rodolfo left me　　　　Fuggì da me stanotte
and said to me: 'All is over'.　　　dicendomi: È finita.
I left the house at day-break　　　A giorno sono uscita
and hurried here　　　　　　　　　e me ne venni a questa
to find him.　　　　　　　　　　volta.

MARCELLO
(watching Rodolfo inside the tavern)

　　　He's waking ... 　　[2]　　Si desta ...
rising and wants me ... he's coming.　　s'alza, mi cerca ... viene.

MIMÌ

He must not see me.　　　　Ch'ei non mi veda!

MARCELLO

Go home at once now,　　　　Or rincasiate ...
Mimì ... for heaven's sake.　　Mimì ... per carità!
Don't make a scene out there!　　non fate scene qua!

(He leads Mimì gently towards the corner of the tavern from where she immediately looks back. Marcello hurries towards Rodolfo.)

RODOLFO
(running towards Marcello) [9]

Marcello, at last I've found you!　　[2, 1]　Marcello. Finalmente!
Here none can hear us.　　　　　Qui niun ci sente.
The time has come for me to　　　Io voglio separarmi da Mimì.
　　leave Mimì.

MARCELLO

Are you sure that is true?　　　Sei volubil così?

RODOLFO

Yes, once before all seemed over,　　Già un'altra volta credetti morto
passion had fled,　　　　　　　il mio cor,
then her blue eyes their glory on me　　ma di quegl'occhi azzurri allo splendor ...
shed ...
Love reawakened.　　　　　　esso è risorto.
Now the torture returns ...　　　Ora il tedio l'assal ...

MARCELLO

Do you wish to recall the pain that's past?　　E gli vuoi rinnovare il funeral?

(Unable to catch every word, Mimì manages to hide behind a plane-tree and so stand nearer the two friends.)

RODOLFO
(sadly)

Yes! always!　　　　Per sempre!

hinking.	Cambia metro.
dull and boring	Dei pazzi è l'amor tetro
in sadness.	che lacrime distilla.
ring joy and gladness	Se non ride e sfavilla
just worthless.	l'amore è fiacco e roco.
But you re jealous.	Tu sei geloso.

RODOLFO

A little.   Un poco.

MARCELLO

Intemperate and changeable, and a victim	Collerico, lunatico, imbevuto
of vile suspicion, impatient and stubborn!	di pregiudizi, noioso, cocciuto!

MIMI
(aside)

(He is making him angry. What shall I do?)	(Or lo fa incollerir! Me poveretta!)

RODOLFO
(with bitter irony)

Mimi is fickle-hearted,	[22] Mimì è una civetta
always flirting with someone. A scented dandy	che frascheggia con tutti. Un moscardino
of noble family	di Viscontino
tries to win her caresses.	le fa l'occhio di triglia.
With shoulders swaying, one tiny foot displaying,	Ella sgonnella e scopre la caviglia
she bestows all the magic of her smile.	con un far promettente e lusinghier ...

MARCELLO

Shall I be frank? You're not being sincere.	Lo devo dir? Non mi sembri sincer.

RODOLFO

Well, you are right. No I'm not. In vain I'm hiding	Ebbene, no, non lo son. Invan nascondo
all the torture that racks me.	la mia vera tortura.
I love Mimì, she is my only treasure, I love her,	Amo Mimì sovra ogni cosa al mondo, io, l'amo,
but oh! I fear it, oh! how I fear it.	ma ho paura, ma ho paura.

(Mimì, astonished, comes closer and closer, under cover of the trees. Rodolfo continues sadly.)

Mimi's so sickly, so ailing!	[23] Mimì è tanto malata!
Every day she grows weaker.	Ogni dì più declina.
That poor unhappy girl,	La povera piccina
is slowly dying!	è condannata!
By fierce incessant coughing	[24] Una terribil tosse
her frail being is shaken,	l'esil petto le scuote,
in her wasted features	già le smunte gote
feverish fires awaken ...	di sangue rosse ...

MARCELLO

Mimì!?!   Mimì!?!

MIMI

What's he saying?   Che vuol dire?

MARCELLO
(agitatedly, perceiving that Mimì is listening)

Oh, our poor Mimì!   Povera Mimì!

MIMI
(weeping)

Alas! I'm dying?   Ahimè, morire?!

RODOLFO

[23]

And my room's but a squalid
    prison cell . . . no fire to warm her . . .
    only the cruel night-wind
        wails cold and cheerless.
She is merry and smiling
    while remorse overwhelms me.
For the fever that wracks her,
    I feel so guilty!
	La mia stanza è una tana
	    squallida . . . il fuoco ho spento
	    V'entra e l'aggira il vento
	        di tramontana.
	Essa canta e sorride,
	    e il rimorso m'assale.
	Me cagion del fatale
	    mal che l'uccide!

MIMÌ
(in anguish)

All is over! Ah me! Ah me! All is over! Life and loving, all are ended! Mimì must die!	O mia vita! Ahimè! Ahimè! È finita! O mia vita! È finita! Ahimè morir!

MARCELLO

What can help her? What can we do? We must help her. Oh, our poor Mimì!	Che far dunque? Oh qual pietà! Poveretta! Povera Mimì!

RODOLFO

Mimì's a hothouse flower.
    Want has wasted her beauty.
    To heal the cruel pain she suffers
        needs more than love.
	Mimì di serra è fiore.
	    Povertà l'ha sfiorita,
	    per richiamarla in vita
	        non basta amor.

(Mimì's violent coughing and sobbing reveal her presence.) [24]

RODOLFO
(seeing Mimì he rushes towards her.)

You! Mimì! You here? You overheard me?	[10] Che? Mimì! Tu qui? M'hai sentito?

MARCELLO

Then she must have been listening!	[6] Ella dunque ascoltava?!

RODOLFO

Surely by now you know me . . . I worry over nothing! Come, let's go inside.	Facile alla paura per nulla io m'arrovello. Vien là nel tepor!

(He tries to take her into the tavern.)

MIMÌ

No, inside there I'd suffocate.	No, quel tanfo mi soffoca!

RODOLFO
(embracing Mimì affectionately)

Ah, Mimì!	Ah, Mimì!

(Musetta's brazen laugh is heard from the tavern.) [16]

MARCELLO

It's Musetta that's laughing.	È Musetta che ride.

(He runs to look through the window)

Laughing, flirting! ah! what a hussy! I'll not allow it!	Con chi ride? Ah, la civetta! Imparerai.

(Furious, he enters the tavern.)

MIMÌ
(disengaging herself from his embrace)

Farewell then.	Addio.

What! Going?	Che! Vai?

MIMI

To the home that she left [10]	D'onde lieta usci
at the voice of her lover,	al tuo grido d'amore,
sad, forsaken Mimì [11]	torna sola Mimì
must turn back heavy-hearted.	al solitario nido.
Once more she'll be returning	Ritorna un'altra volta
to tend her lifeless flowers.	a intesser finti fior.
Farewell, then, I wish you well!	Addio, senza rancor!
Just one more favour.	Ascolta, ascolta.
Gather these few poor things I left	Le poche robe aduna che lasciai
there behind me. Inside my trunk	sparse. Nel mio cessetto
you will find them. That small chain	stan chiusi quel cerchietto d'or,
of gold,	
the prayer book you gave me. [12b]	e il libro di preghiere.
Please put them all together safe in	Involgi tutto quanto in un grembiale
my apron,	
I will send round to fetch them ...	e manderò il portiere ...
Dearest, under the pillow you'll find	Bada, sotto il guanciale c'è la cuffietta
my little bonnet.	rosa.
Who knows? ... Maybe ... you'd like to	Se vuoi ... se vuoi ... serbarla a
keep it to remember our love!	ricordo d'amor!
Goodbye then.	Addio,
Goodbye, I wish you well!	addio, senza rancor ...

RODOLFO

Then at last all is over.	Dunque è proprio finita?
You are going, yes, you're going, my little	Te ne vai, te ne vai, la mia piccina?!
darling.	
Farewell, O sweet dream of love!	Addio, sogni d'amor!
Farewell to our dreamy existence! ...	Addio sognante vita ...
enlivened by your smiling! ...	che un tuo sorriso acquieta!

MIMI

Farewell, awaking beside you [26]	Addio, dolce svegliare
when the day is breaking!	alla mattina!
(playfully)	
Farewell to jealousy and anger!	Addio, rabbuffi e gelosie!
Farewell suspicion!	Sospetti!

RODOLFO

Kisses!	Baci!

MIMI

... and all its bitter sadness.	... pungenti amarezze!

RODOLFO

... which as lover and poet	... ch'io da vero poeta
I rhymed with joy and gladness.	rimavo con: carezze!

RODOLFO, MIMI

Lonely in winter with death as sole [27]	Soli d'inverno è cosa da morire!
companion!	
Yet the lovely springtime brings the	Mentre a primavera c'è compagno il sol!
glorious sun!	

(*In the tavern can be heard the sound of breaking plates and glasses, and the voices of Musetta and Marcello.*)

[25]

MARCELLO

I can guess what you were doing.	Che facevi? Che dicevi
You were flirting with that stranger.	presso al fuoco a quel signore?

MUSETTA

What do you mean?   Che vuoi dir?

(Musetta runs out angrily; Marcello follows her and stops at the door.)

MIMI

I'm not lonely in spring.   Niuno è solo l'april.

MARCELLO

    And how you coloured   Al mio venire
when I caught you in the corner.   Hai mutato di colore.

MUSETTA

That poor fellow simply asked me: Quel signore mi diceva:
    'Are you very fond of dancing?'   Ama il ballo signorina?
    I was blushing when I answered: Arrossendo rispondeva:
    'I'd be dancing all day long, sir.' Ballerei sera a mattina.

RODOLFO

As comrades you've lilies and roses ... Si parla coi gigli e le rose ...

MIMI

Forth from each nest there comes a gentle   Esce dai nidi un cinguettio gentile.
    murmur.

MARCELLO

This is talk that only   Quel discorso asconde
    leads to things dishonest;   mire disoneste.
    I will teach you better manners   Io t'acconcio per le feste
    if I catch you once more flirting! se ti colgo a incivettire!

MUSETTA

I will do just what I like!   Voglio piena libertà!
What a bother!   Chè mi canti?

RODOLFO, MIMI

When the hawthorn bough's in blossom Al fiorir di primavera
we've the glorious sun!   c'è compagno il sol!
Silvery fountains murmur ...   Chiacchieran le fontane ...
The breezes of the evening   La brezza della sera
bring hope and solace, calming human balsami stende sulle doglie umane.
    sorrow.
Shall we then await for Spring to come Vuoi che aspettiam la primavera ancor?
    again?

MUSETTA

Why this anger? Why this fury?   Chè mi gridi? Chè mi canti?
We're not married yet, thank goodness! All'altar non siamo uniti.
I detest that sort of lover   Io detesto quegli amanti
who pretends he is ... ha! ha! ... your che la fanno da ... ah! ah! ... mariti!
    husband!
I shall flirt just when it suits me. Fo' all'amor con chi mi piace,
Yes, your lordship,   Non ti garba?
Musetta's going away, yes, going away! Musetta se ne va, si, se ne va!
                    (ironically)
Fare you well, sir. Good sir, farewell, Vi saluto. Signor, addio
farewell with all my heart!   vi dico con piacer!

MARCELLO

You shall not do as you like, Miss,   Bada, sotto il mio cappello
I'm the master, don't forget it.   non ci stan certi ornamenti.
I'm not going to be your plaything   Io non faccio da zimbello
just because you're fond of flirting. ai novizi intraprendenti.
You're most frivolous, Musetta.   Vana, frivola, civetta.
So you're going, God be with you   Ve n'andate? Vi ringrazio:
and for me 'tis a good riddance.   or son ricco divenuto.

(ironically)

Fare you well, Ma'am.	Vi saluto.
Farewell, Ma'am, pray begone.	Son servo e me ne vo'!

MUSETTA
(She retreats in a fury; but suddenly stops and shouts her last words at him.)

Go back and paint your house!	Pittore de bottega!

MARCELLO

Rattlesnake!	Vipera!

MUSETTA

Amateur!	Rospo!

(She departs.)

MARCELLO

Bitch!	Strega!

(He enters the tavern.)

MIMI
(moving away with Rodolfo)

Always yours . . . for ever!	Sempre tua . . . per la vita!

RODOLFO

We'll be together till the Spring returns!	Ci lasceremo alla stagion dei fior . . .

MIMI

Ah, that our winter	Vorrei che eterno
might last for ever!	durasse il verno!

BOTH
(off-stage)

We part no more	Ci lascierem
until the Spring returns.	alla stagion dei fior!

Curtain.

... At that period, indeed for some time past, the friends had lived lonely lives.

Musetta had once more become a sort of semi-official personage; for three or four months Marcello had not seen her.

And Mimì too; no word of her had Rodolfo heard, except he talked about her to himself when he was alone.

One day, as Marcello furtively kissed a bunch of ribbons that Musetta had left behind, he saw Rodolfo hiding away a bonnet, that same pink bonnet which Mimì had forgotten.

'Good!' muttered Marcello, 'he's as craven-hearted as I.'

. . . . .
. . . . .

A gay life, yet a terrible one!

La Bohème at Covent Garden in 1902, the season in which Melba and Caruso first sang as Mimì and Rodolfo in London together, establishing the opera firmly in the repertory. L. to R. Parkina, Gilibert, Caruso, Scotti, Journet. (Raymond Mander and Joe Mitchenson Theatre Collection)

Act Four

In the Attic.

Marcello — Rodolfo

(Marcello, as before, stands in front of his easel, while Rodolfo is seated at his writing-table; each trying to convince the other he is working tirelessly, whereas both are really only gossiping.) [1]

MARCELLO
(resuming his talk)

In a coupé?   In un coupé?

RODOLFO

    In a carriage and pair, [15]   Con pariglia e livree.
she greeted me so gaily. Well, 'Musetta!'   Mi salutò ridendo. Tò, Musetta!
I asked her, 'How's your heart?' 'It's   Le dissi: — e il cuor? — 'Non batte o non lo
silent, or I don't feel it, [16]   sento,
thanks to this velvet that covers it.'   grazie al velluto che il copre'.

MARCELLO
(trying to laugh)

    Delighted   Ci ho gusto
to hear it.   davver.

RODOLFO
(aside)

    (You can't fool me. You're fretting   (Loiola, va. Ti rodi e ridi.)
and fuming.)

MARCELLO
(pondering)

It's silent. Bravo!   Non batte? Bene!
(He begins to paint again.)
    And I noticed . . .   Io pur vidi . . .

RODOLFO

    Musetta?   Musetta?

MARCELLO

Mimì. .   Mimì.

RODOLFO
(breathlessly)

    You saw her?   L'hai vista?
(recovering his composure)
    How curious!   Oh, guarda!

MARCELLO
(stopping his work)

    Out in her carriage, [10]   Era in carrozza
arrayed in splendour just like a duchess.   vestita come una regina.

RODOLFO

    Delightful!   Evviva!
I'm glad to hear it.   Ne son contento.

MARCELLO
(aside)

    (You liar, you're pining   (Bugiardo, si strugge
with love.)   d'amor.)

RODOLFO

Now, to work.   Lavoriam.

MARCELLO

Now, to work.   Lavoriam.

(They go on working.)

RODOLFO
(He throws down his pen.)

The pen is useless!   Che penna infame!
(He remains seated, apparently lost in thought.)

MARCELLO
(He flings away his brush.)

This infamous paint-brush!   Che infame pennello!
(He stares at his canvas, and then, without Rodolfo noticing he takes a bunch of ribbons from his pocket, and kisses it.)

RODOLFO

Mimì, our love is over.	[28] Mimì, tu più non torni.
Oh days departed,	O giorni belli,
hands pale and slender, and soft fragrant tresses! . . .	piccole mani — odorosi capelli . . .
Ah, snowy forehead! Ah, the golden days of youth.	collo di neve! Ah Mimì, mia breve gioventù!
And you, her little bonnet,	E tu, cuffietta lieve,
she left you behind the day she departed,	che sotto il guancial partendo ascose
you recall the days of our youth and joy,	tutta sai la nostra felicità,
come to my heart,	vien sul mio cuor!
lie close against my heart, since my love is dead.	Ah vien sul mio cuor; poichè è morto amor!

(Rodolfo clasps the bonnet to his heart.)

MARCELLO
(putting the ribbons away, he again stares at the canvas)

I know not how this brush	Io non so come sia
of mine continues to labour	che il mio pennello lavori
and paints on these colours	e impasti colori
quite against my will.	contro voglia mia.
And though I would be painting	Se pingere mi piace
fields and meadows in winter or in spring-time,	o cieli o terre o inverni o primavere,
here on my canvas two bright eyes torment me,	egli mi traccia due pupille nere
and two red smiling lips.	e una bocca procace,
The features of Musetta haunt me still!	e n'esce di Musetta il viso ancor!
Ah! here I see Musetta	e n'esce di Musetta
so fair and so alluring, so deceiving.	il viso tutto vezzi e tutto frode.
My grief affords her pleasure	Musetta intanto gode
yet my foolish heart longs to call her name and hold her in my arms.	e il mio cuor vile la chiama e aspetta il vil mio cuor.

RODOLFO
(trying to hide his emotion from Marcello, he carelessly asks)

What is the time now?   Che ora sia?

MARCELLO
(roused from his reverie, he gaily replies)

Time for yesterday's dinner.   L'ora del pranzo . . . di ieri.

RODOLFO

And Schaunard's not back yet?   E Schaunard no torna?

97

(*Enter Schaunard and Colline; the former with four rolls, the latter with a paper bag.*) [4]

SCHAUNARD

Here we are.   Eccoci.
(*He places the rolls on the table.*)

RODOLFO, MARCELLO

Well then?   Ebben?

MARCELLO
(*disdainfully*)

Some bread?   Del pan?

COLLINE
(*taking a herring from the bag*)

A dish that's worthy of Demosthenes: È un piatto degno di Demostene:
a herring!   un'aringa . . .

SCHAUNARD

It's salted!   . . . salata.

COLLINE

The meal is ready now.   Il pranzo è in tavola.

(*Seating themselves around the table, they pretend to be having a fine meal.*)

MARCELLO

This is a food that's   Questa è cuccagna
fit for a banquet.   da Berlingaccio.

SCHAUNARD
(*He places Colline's hat on the table and thrusts a bottle of water into it.*)

Now we must put the   Or lo sciampagna
Champagne on ice.   mettiamo in ghiaccio.

RODOLFO
(*to Marcello, offering him some bread*)

Choose, Royal Highness,   Scelga, o Barone;
lobster or salmon?   trota o salmone?

MARCELLO
(*to Schaunard, offering another crust of bread*)

Baron, here's a nightingale's Duca, una lingua
tongue in brandy.   di pappagallo?

SCHAUNARD

Thank you, I dare not!   Grazie, m'impingua.
This evening I'm dancing.   Stassera ho un ballo.

(*The one and only tumbler is handed round. Colline rises when he has devoured his bread.*)

RODOLFO
(*to Colline*)

What? Finished?   Già sazio?

COLLINE
(*with an air of great importance*) [3]

To business.   Ho fretta.
The king awaits me.   Il Re m'aspetta.

MARCELLO
(*eagerly*)

What plot is brewing?   C'è qualche trama?

RODOLFO

What's going on?   Qualche mister?

SCHAUNARD
(rising and asking with comic curiosity)

What's in the wind?   Qualche mister?

COLLINE
(strutting up and down, full of self-importance)

The king requires me   Il Re mi chiama
at his side.   al minister.

SCHAUNARD
(to Marcello)

Bravo!   Bene!

MARCELLO

Bravo!   Bene!

RODOLFO

Bravo!   Bene!

COLLINE
(with a patronising air)

And then ...   Però ...
I go to see Guizot!   vedrò ... vedrò Guizot!

SCHAUNARD
(to Marcello)

Give me a goblet!   Porgimi il nappo!

SCHAUNARD
(He hands him the only glass.)

Ho! Quaff now a bumper!   Sì! Bevi, io pappo!

SCHAUNARD
(solemnly, getting on a chair and raising the glass)

Unaccustomed as I am to   Mi sia permesso — al nobile
    public speaking ...   consesso ...

RODOLFO
(interrupting)

Stop that!   Basta!

MARCELLO

Stupid!   Fiacco!

COLLINE

No more fooling!   Che decotto!

MARCELLO

No more nonsense!   Leva il tacco!

COLLINE

Give me that tumbler!   Dammi il gotto!

SCHAUNARD
(motioning his friends to let him speak; in rapture)

With ardour irresistible   M'ispira irresistibile
Poetry fills my spirit ...   l'estro della romanza ...

OTHERS
(yelling)

No!   No!

SCHAUNARD
(complacently)

Then something choreographic   Azione coreografica
may suit you ...   allora? ...

(*amid applause, Schaunard gets off the chair*)

Yes! . . .   Sì! . . .

SCHAUNARD

Some dancing,   La danza
accompanied by singing!   con musica vocale!

COLLINE

Let's clear the stage for action!   Si sgombrino le sale!

(*moving table and chairs aside, they prepare for a dance. They suggest various dances.*)

Gavotta.   Gavotta.

MARCELLO

Minuetto.   Minuetto.

SCHAUNARD

Pavanella.   Pavanella.

RODOLFO
(*imitating a Spanish measure*)

Fandango.   Fandango.

COLLINE

I vote we dance quadrilles.   [29]   Propongo la quadriglia.
(*The others approve.*)

RODOLFO

Here's to the ladies.   Mano alle dame.

COLLINE

I'll call it.   Io detto.

SCHAUNARD

Lallera, lallera, là.   Lallera, lallera, là.
(*improvising, he beats time with comic pomposity*)

RODOLFO
(*bowing to Marcello, with great gallantry*)

Oh, maiden fair and gentle!   Vezzosa damigella . . .

MARCELLO
(*coyly bashful, imitating a woman's voice*)

My modesty respect, Sir,   Risepetti la modestia,
I beg you!   la prego.
(*Rodolfo and Marcello dance a minuet.*)

COLLINE
(*leading the dancing*)

Balancez!   Balancez!

SCHAUNARD
(*teasing*)

Lallera, lallera, là.   Lallera, lallera, là.
First there's the Round.   Prima c'è il *Rond*.

COLLINE

No, stupid!!   No, bestia!!

SCHAUNARD
(*with exaggerated contempt*)

You've manners like a clown!   Che modi da lacchè!

COLLINE
(*offended*)

As I take it,   Se non erro

you're insulting!   lei m'oltraggia!
Draw your sword, sir!   Snudi il ferro!
(He seizes the tongs from the stove.)

SCHAUNARD
(He picks up the poker.)

Ready!   Pronti!
(He attacks.)
On guard there.   Assaggia.
(preparing to receive his adversary's attack)
Only blood my thirst will quell.   Il tuo sangue lo voglio ber.

COLLINE

One of us shall now be gutted!   Un di noi qui si sbudella.

SCHAUNARD

Go and get a stretcher ready!   Apprestate una barella.

COLLINE

And prepare a grave as well.   Apprestate un cimiter.

(Schaunard and Colline duel. As they fight, Marcello and Rodolfo dance around them singing.)

RODOLFO AND MARCELLO

While they beat each   Mentre incalza
other's brains out,   la tenzone
our fandango   gira e balza
we will finish.   Rigodone.

Musetta — later Mimì

(The duellists pretend to grow more incensed, stamping and shouting. The door opens and Musetta enters in a state of great agitation.)

MARCELLO
(seeing her)

Musetta!   Musetta!

(All are amazed.)

MUSETTA
(hoarsely)

It's Mimì ...   C'è Mimì ...

(They anxiously cluster round Musetta.)

It's Mimì who is with me and is ailing.   C'è Mimì che mi segue e che sta male.

RODOLFO

Mimì?   Ov'è?

MUSETTA

She has not strength   Nel far le scale
to climb up the staircase.   più non si resse.

(Through the open door he sees Mimì seated on the topmost stair.)

RODOLFO

Ah!   Ah!
(He rushes to Mimì; Marcello follows his example.) [10, 6]

SCHAUNARD
(to Colline, as they pull the bed forward)

Let   Noi
her rest here for a moment.   accostiamo quel lettuccio.

RODOLFO
(Rodolfo and Marcello support Mimì and lead her towards the bed, gently lowering her on to it.) [11]

There!   Là.

Some water.

(to his companions, softly)

Da bere.

(Musetta brings a glass of water and makes Mimì sip it.)

MIMI

(Recovering slightly, she is aware of Rodolfo beside her.)

Rodolfo!   Rodolfo!

RODOLFO

Gently, lie down there.   Zitta, riposa.

MIMI

My dear Rodolfo, oh let me   O mio Rodolfo, mi vuoi
stay with you!   qui con te?

RODOLFO

(With deep affection he bids Mimì to remain silent and stays by her side.)

Darling Mimì, now and always!   Ah! mia Mimì, sempre! sempre!

MUSETTA

(to Marcello, Schaunard and Colline, softly)

I heard them saying that Mimì had fled   Intesi dire che Mimì, fuggita
from her noble lover and now was almost   dal Viscontino, era in fin di vita.
    dying.
Ah, but where? Searching, searching, I met   Dove stia? Cerca, cerca ... la veggo
    her
alone just now,   passar per via ...
almost dead with exhaustion.   trascinandosi a stento.
She murmured: 'I am dying ...   Mi dice: 'Più non reggo ...
dying, dying! But listen!   Muoio, muoio, lo sento ...
I want to die near him; perhaps he's   Voglio morir con lui ... Forse
    waiting ...   m'aspetta ...
Take me to him, Musetta ...'   M'accompagni, Musetta? ...'

MARCELLO

(He motions Musetta to talk softly.)

Hush!   Sst.

MIMI

I feel so much better ...   Mi sento assai meglio ...
all here seems just the same as ever.   lascia ch'io guardi intorno.
(with a sweet smile)
Ah! I'm so happy to be here   Ah! come si sta bene qui!
I feel better ... Once more new life   Si rinasce ... Ancor sento la vita!
    returns to me.
(raising herself, she embraces Rodolfo)
No, beloved do not go!   No, tu non mi lasci più!

RODOLFO

Oh my love, my treasure,   Benedetta bocca
once more enchant me! ...   tu ancor mi parli! ...

MUSETTA

(to the three)

What is there   Che ci avete
to give her?   in casa?

MARCELLO

Nothing!   Nulla!

MUSETTA

Any wine, or coffee?   Non caffè? Non vino?

MARCELLO

(in great dejection)

Nothing! There is nothing!   Nulla! Ah! miseria!

102

SCHAUNARD
(*sadly to Colline as he takes him aside*)

Half an hour she'll be dead.	Fra mezz'ora è morta!

MIMI

I feel so cold . . .	Ho tanto freddo . . .
I wish I had my muff here!	Se avessi un manicotto!
My poor hands are simply frozen, how shall I get them warm?	Queste mie mani riscaldare non si potranno mai?

(*She coughs.*)

ROLDOLFO
(*He takes Mimi's hands in his and chafes them.*)

In mine, in mine, love!	Qui, nelle mie, taci!
Please, do not speak, it tires you.	Il parlar ti stanca.

MIMI

It is the coughing!	Ho un po' di tosse!
I'm used to that, though.	Ci sono avvezza.

(*Seeing Rodolfo's friends, she calls them by name; they hasten to her side.*)

Good morning, Marcello,	Buon giorno, Marcello,
Schaunard, Colline, good morning!	Schaunard, Colline, buon giorno.
All are here, all are here	Tutti qui, tutti qui
glad to welcome Mimì.	sorridenti a Mimì.

RODOLFO

Hush, Mimì, do not talk.	Non parlar, non parlar.

MIMI

I'll speak low.	Parlo pian,
Don't be frightened. Marcello, let me tell you:	non temere. Marcello, date retta:
She is good, your Musetta.	è assai buona Musetta.

MARCELLO
(*He gives his hand to Musetta.*)

I know, I know.	Lo so, lo so.

(*Schaunard and Colline mournfully withdraw; the former sits at the table, his head in his hands; the latter is a prey to sad thoughts.*)

MUSETTA
(*She takes off her earrings, gives them to Marcello and whispers:*)

Look here, sell them, and buy her something to drink; send for a doctor! . . .	A te, vendi, riporta qualche cordial, manda un dottore! . . .

RODOLFO

To sleep now.	Riposa.

MIMI

You will not leave me?	Tu non mi lasci?

(*Mimì gradually grows drowsy, and Rodolfo takes a chair and sits by the bed.*)

RODOLFO

No.	No.

MUSETTA

But listen!	Ascolta!
Maybe what she has asked us will be her last request on earth, little darling!	[16] Forse è l'ultima volta che ha espresso un desiderio, poveretta!
I'll go and fetch the muff. I'll come with you.	Pel manicotto io vo. Con te verrò.

MARCELLO
(*greatly moved*)

How good you are, Musetta!	Sei buona, o mia Musetta.

(Musetta and Marcello hurry out.)

COLLINE

(...tta and Marcello are talking Colline has removed his overcoat. He addresses it ...ing emotion.)

...ble garment, listen. [30]	Vecchia zimarra, senti,
...goodbye, for we	io resto al pian, tu ascendere
from each other must be parted ...	il sacro monte o devi ...
Noble friend, I salute you.	Le mie grazie ricevi.
These faded shoulders never deigned	Mai non curvasti il logoro
to bow to rich man or to mighty;	dorso ai ricchi, ai potenti.
Often, deep in these pockets,	Passar nelle tue tasche
you have sheltered in silence	come in antri tranquilli
philosophers and poets.	filosofi e poeti.
Now that our pleasant friendship	Ora che i giorni lieti
is over, I bid you farewell then,	fuggir, ti dico: addio,
companion tried and trusty.	fedele amico mio.
Farewell! Farewell!	Addio! addio!

(Colline folds up the coat and puts it under his arm, but seeing Schaunard says to him softly:)

Schaunard, quite possibly our methods differ,	Schaunard, ognuno per diversa via
but now together two kindly acts we'll do:	mettiamo insieme due atti di pietà;
mine's this one!	io ... questo!

(pointing to the coat under his arm)

And your's ...	È tu ...

(looking towards Rodolfo at Mimì's bedside)

... leave them alone in here ...	... lasciali soli là! ...

SCHAUNARD
(overcome with emotion.)

Philosopher, you're right! [4]	Filosofo, ragioni!
You're right! ... I'll go!	È ver! ... Vo via!

(Schaunard looks about him; then, to justify his exit, he picks up the water-bottle and goes out after Colline, gently closing the door.)

Mimì — Rodolfo

MIMI [9]
(opening her eyes, she sees the others have gone and holds out her hand to Rodolfo who kisses it affectionately.)

Have they left us? I was not really sleeping, [31]	Sono andati? Fingevo di dormire ...
but I wanted to be alone with you, love.	perchè volli con te sola restare.
So many things remain for me to tell you ...	Ho tante cose che ti voglio dire ...
or just one too, as spacious as the ocean,	o una sola, ma grande come il mare,
as the ocean so deep and never ending ...	come il mare profonda ed infinita ...

(embracing him)

You are my love, and all in life I treasure.	Sei il mio amor e tutta la mia vita.

RODOLFO

Oh, my lovely Mimì!	O mia bella Mimì!

MIMI
(letting her arms drop)

You still think I'm pretty?	Son bella ancora?

RODOLFO

Fair as dawn in the Springtime.	Bella come un'aurora.

MIMI

No, no, you are mistaken.	Hai sbagliato il raffronto.
You meant to say: fair as sunset in autumn.	Volevi dir: bella come un tramonto.
'I'm always called Mimì ... [10]	'Mi chiamano Mimì ...
but I know not why.'	il perchè non so.'

RODOLFO
(in tender caressing tones)

Back to her nest comes the swallow in the [12] Tornò al nido la rondine e cinguetta.
Springtime.

(He takes out the bonnet and gives it to Mimì.)

MIMI
(gaily)

My little bonnet.   La mia cuffietta.
(She motions Rodolfo to put the bonnet on her head. She rests her head on his breast.)
Do you remember how we met that evening,   Te lo rammenti quando sono entrata
when I by chance came here?   la prima volta, là?

RODOLFO

Yes, I remember!   Se lo rammento!

MIMI

This room was all in darkness ...   Il lume s'era spento ...

RODOLFO

You were anxious and frightened!   Eri tanto turbata!
Then the key you'd mislaid, love ...   [7]   Poi smarristi la chiave ...

MIMI

And in the darkness you tried so hard   E a cercarla tastoni ti sei
to find it.   messo!

RODOLFO

Yes, searching, searching ...   E cerca, cerca ...

MIMI

You, my fine young poet,   Mio bel signorino,
now I can tell you frankly   posso ben dirlo adesso,
that you soon managed to find it.   lei la trovò assai presto.

RODOLFO

Fate and I worked together.   Aiutavo il destino.

MIMI
(remembering her first meeting with Rodolfo on Christmas Eve)

It was dark, and all my blushes were   Era buio; il mio rossor non si vedeva ...
unnoticed ...
(she faintly repeats Rodolfo's words.)
'Your tiny hand is frozen!...   [8]   'Che gelida manina ...
let me warm it into life!...'   se la lasci riscaldar!...'
It was dark and you took my hand so   Era buio, e la man tu mi prendevi ...
gently.
(A sudden spasm half suffocates Mimì; she sinks back fainting.) [6]

RODOLFO
(raising her up in alarm)

Oh God! Mimì!   Oh Dio! Mimì!

(At this moment Schaunard returns and hearing Rodolfo's exclamation, hurries to Mimì's bedside.)

SCHAUNARD

What's wrong?   Che avvien?

MIMI
(She opens her eyes and smilingly reassures Rodolfo and Schaunard.)

Nothing. I'm better.   Nulla. Sto bene.

RODOFLO

Gently, take care, I pray.   Zitta, per carità.

Yes, yes, forgive me.   Sì, sì, perdona.

Now I'm better.   Or sarò buona.

Musetta — Marcello — later Colline

(Musetta and Marcello enter. Musetta is carrying a muff, her companion a phial.)

MUSETTA
(to Rodolfo)

Sleeping?   Dorme?

RODOLFO

Just resting.   Riposa.

MARCELLO

I have just seen the doctor!   Ho veduto il dottore!
He'll come; I made him hurry.   Verrà; gli ho fatto fretta.
Here is the medicine.   Ecco il cordiale.
(He takes a spirit-lamp and, placing it on the table, lights it.)

MIMI

Who is it?   Chi parla?

MUSETTA
(She approaches Mimì and gives her the muff.)

I, Musetta.   Io, Musetta.

MIMI
(Helped by Musetta, she sits up in bed and with almost childlike glee seizes the muff.)

Oh, see how soft and warm it is. No more [8b]   Oh, come è bello e morbido! Non più
my fingers will be frozen. For this muff   le mani allividite ora. Il tepore
will keep them warm.   le abbellirà.
(to Rodolfo)
Did you give me this present?   Sei tu che me lo doni?

MUSETTA
(eagerly)

Yes.   Sì.

MIMI

You! What a spendthrift!   Tu! Spensierato!
Thank you. It cost you dear. Weep not! I'm   Grazie. Ma costerà. Piangi? Sto bene ...
better ...
Why should you weep like this? ...   Pianger così perchè?
(She thrusts her hands in the muff, then she gradually grows drowsy, gracefully nodding her head as she is overcome by sleep.)
My love ... always with you! ...   Qui ... amor ... sempre con te! ...
My hands are ... much warmer;   Le mani ... al caldo ... e ... dormire.
and ... I'll sleep now.

(Silence.)

RODOLFO
(to Marcello)

What did   Che ha detto
the doctor say?   il medico?

MARCELLO

He'll come.   Verrà.

MUSETTA
(She is busily heating the medicine over the spirit-lamp, as she unconciously murmurs a prayer.)

Oh Mary, blessed Virgin,   Madonna benedetta,
look down in mercy on a soul that suffers.   fate la grazia a questa poveretta

| Grant that death may not take her. | che non debba morire. |

(interrupting herself, to Marcello)

| There should be some protection | Qui ci vuole un riparo |
| because the light is troubling her. | perchè la fiamma sventola. |

(Marcello places a book upright on the table so as to shade the lamp.)

| That's right. | Così. |

(resuming her prayer)

Grant that she may recover.	E che possa guarire.
Most Holy Mother, I am not	Madonna santa, io sono
worthy of forgiveness,	indegna di perdono,
but our little Mimì's	mentre invece Mimì
an angel come from heaven.	è un angelo del cielo.

(Rodolfo approaches Musetta as she is praying.)

RODOLFO

| I still have hope. Do you think it can be serious? | Io spero ancora. Vi pare che sia grave? |

MUSETTA

| Not serious. | Non credo. |

SCHAUNARD
(He advances on tip-toe to the bedside. With a sorrowful gesture he goes back to Marcello.)

| Marcello, she is dead ... | Marcello, è spirata ... |

(Marcello in his turn goes up to the bed and retreats in alarm; Colline enters and puts some money on the table near Musetta. A ray of sunshine falls through the window upon Mimì's face; Musetta points to her cloak which Rodolfo takes, with a grateful glance. Standing on a chair, he tries to form a screen by stretching it across the window-pane.)

COLLINE
(to Musetta)

| Musetta, for you. | Musetta, a voi! |

(He hurries to help Rodolfo stretch the cloak across the window, as he asks after Mimì.)

| How is she? | Come va? ... |

RODOLFO

| Look there. She is sleeping. | Vedi? ... È tranquilla. |

(He turns to Mimì; at that moment Musetta makes a sign to him that the medicine is ready. He suddenly becomes aware of the strange demeanour of Marcello and Schaunard who look at each other in great sadness. Huskily, almost in a speaking voice, he asks:)

What's the matter?	Che vuol dire
Why all this coming and going?	quell'andare e venire ...
Why do you look at me like that?	quel guardarmi così ...

(He glances from one to the other in consternation.)

MARCELLO
(Unable to bear up any longer, he embraces Rodolfo, as he murmurs:)

| Have courage! | Coraggio! |

RODOLFO [31]
(He throws himself on the bed, lifts Mimì's body, strokes her hand and cries out in anguish:)

| Mimì! ... Mimì! ... | Mimì! ... Mimì! ... |

(He falls sobbing on her lifeless form. Terror struck, Musetta rushes to the bed, utters a piercing cry of grief; then she kneels, sobbing, at the foot of the bed; Schaunard, overcome, sinks back into a chair; to the left, Colline stands at the foot of the bed, dazed at the suddenness of this catastrophe; Marcello, sobbing, turns his back to the footlights. The curtain falls slowly.)

The death of Mimi at Covent Garden in the 1982 televised performance (photo: Reg Wilson)

Discography / *Martin Hoyle* All complete recordings are in stereo (unless asterisked*) and in Italian. The enthusiast is also referred to Alan Blyth's *Opera on Record* (Hutchinson 1979). This discography includes only recordings currently available in the UK or USA.

Conductor Company/Orchestra	Beecham RCA Victor	Votto La Scala, Milan	Serafin Sta Cecilia	Levine National Phil, Ambrosian Op. Chorus	Solti Alldis Cho. LPO
Rodolfo	Björling	Di Stefano	Bergonzi	Kraus	Domingo
Mimi	De los Angeles	Callas	Tebaldi	Scotto	Caballé
Musetta	Amara	Moffo	d'Angelo	Neblett	Blegen
Marcello	Merrill	Panerai	Bastianini	Milnes	Milnes
Colline	Tozzi	Zaccaria	Siepi	Plishka	Raimondi
Schaunard	Reardon	Spatafora	Cesari	Manuguerra	Sardinero
Benoit	Corena	Badioli	Corena	Tajo	Mangin
Alcindoro	Corena	Badioli	Corena	Capecchi	Castel
Disc UK number	SLS896	SLS5059	D5D2	SLS5192	ARL2-0371
Tape UK number	TC-SLS896	TC-SLS5059	K5K22	TC-SLS5192	ARD2-0371
Excerpts (Disc)	ESD7023	SLS856	JB11		
Excerpts (Tape)	TC-ESD7023		KJBC11		
Disc US number	S6099	Angel 3560BL	LON1208	SZBX-3900	ARL2-0371
Tape US number	4X2G-6099		LON25201		
Excerpts (Disc) US			525201		
Excerpts (Tape) US					

109

Conductor Company/Orchestra	*Schippers* Rome Opera	*Karajan* Berlin Opera	*Davis* Royal Opera	*Votto* Maggio Musicale
Rodolfo	Gedda	Pavarotti	Carreras	Poggi
Mimi	Freni	Freni	Ricciarelli	Scotto
Musetta	Adani	Harwood	Putnam	Meneguzzer
Marcello	Sereni	Panerai	Wixell	Gobbi
Colline	Mazzoli	Ghiaurov	Lloyd	Modesti
Schaunard	Basiola	Maffeo	Hagegård	Giorgetti
Benoit	Badioli	Senéchal	de Angelis	Carbonari
Alcindoro	Montarsolo	Senéchal	Elvin	Carbonari
Disc UK number	SLS907	SET565-6	6769 031	DG2705038
Tape UK number	TG-SLS907	K2A5	7600 116	
Excerpts (disc)		SET579		
Excerpts (tape)				
Disc US number	S3643	LON 1299	6769 031	2726086
Tape US number		5-1299	7699 116	3372086
Excerpts (disc) US	S36199	26399		
Excerpts (tape) US	36199	5-26399		

Excerpts UK numbers only are given

Number	Artist	Disc	Tape
Che gelida manina	Pavarotti	D253D2	K253K22
"	Bergonzi	SPA535	KCS535
"	Dvorsky	91120544	
"	Bonisolli	DC21723	
"	Aragall	DC29391	
"	Gedda		TC2-MOM112
"	Caruso	RL11749	RK11749
"	McCormack	SH399	TC-SH399
"	Schipa	GEMM192	
"	Tauber (*in German*)	GEMM214	
Sì, mi chiamano Mimì	Freni	DC29384	DF39384
"	Arroyo	DC23325	
"	Callas	ALP3799	TC-ALP3799
"	Tebaldi	SDD481	KSDC481
"	Caballé	ASD26326	
"	Lorengar	CC7530	CCT7530
"	Cotrubas	76521	
"	Mitchell	SXL6942	
Musetta's waltz song	Welitsch	SH289	
"	Zeani	CC7530	CCT7530
"	Scotto	76407	76407
"	Kabaivanska	RL31475	
O soave fanciulla	Freni, Pavarotti	D25D32	K253K22
"	Freni, Bonisolli	DC29384	DF39384
"	Melba, Caruso	SXL6832	
O Mimì, ti più non torni	Björling, Merrill	RL43243	RK43243
"	Caruso, Scotti	GV542	
"	Gigli, Ruffo	GEMM202-6	
Highlights	Hammond, Craig	ESD7033	TC-ESD7033

Bibliography

Mosco Carner has written *Puccini: A Critical Biography* (Duckworth, 1974) which combines rare psychological insight with musical scholarship. It is laid out in three parts (*The Man, The Artist, The Work*) to give a masterly and very readable survey of every aspect of the subject. Edward Greenfield has written *Puccini: Keeper of the Seal* (London, 1958), and William Ashbrook has written *The Operas of Puccini* (Cassell, 1969).

Scènes de la vie de bohème by Henry Murger has been republished (in French) by Editions D'Aujourd'hui in 1979 (a reprint of the 1861 text). It is not readily available although there have been translations by Ellen Marriage and John Selwyn, and by Elizabeth W. Hughes (Liberal World Literature Series: Hyperion, 1978, USA). Robert Baldick's *The First Bohemian: The Life of Henry Murger* (London, 1961), in which Murger's Paris is described and discussed, is highly recommended.

Puccini's letters (edited and translated by Adami, 1974) are also of interest.

Contributors

William Ashbrook, Professor of English and Humanities at Indiana State University, is the author of *Donizetti, The Operas of Puccini* and a forthcoming Cambridge Opera Handbook on *Turandot*.

Nicholas John is Editorial Co-ordinator for English National Opera and the author of 'Opera' to be published in the *Topics in Music* series by Oxford University Press.

Edward Greenfield, chief music critic of *The Guardian*, is co-author of the *Penguin Stereo Music Guide*, a contributor to *The Gramophone* since 1960 and a regular broadcaster in records and music for the BBC.

Joanna Richardson is a specialist in French studies and the biographer of Théophile Gautier, Princess Mathilde and Verlaine.